# Jelly Roll
## Inspirations

COMPILED BY
### Pam and Nicky Lintott

D&C
David and Charles
www.rucraft.co.uk

A DAVID & CHARLES BOOK
Copyright © David & Charles Limited 2009

David & Charles is an F+W Media Inc. company
4700 East Galbraith Road
Cincinnati, OH 45236

First published in the UK and US in 2009

Text and designs copyright © Pam Lintott and Nicky Lintott 2009
Layout and photography copyright © David & Charles 2009

A catalogue record for this book is available from the British Library.

ISBN-10: 978-0-7153-3311-2 paperback
ISBN-13: 0-7153-3311-9 paperback

Printed in China by RR Donnelley
for David & Charles
Brunel House   Newton Abbot   Devon

Commissioning Editor  Jane Trollope
Editorial Manager  Emily Pitcher
Assistant Editor  Kate Nicholson
Project Editor  Lin Clements
Art Editor  Sarah Clark
Designer  Sarah Underhill
Production Controller  Kelly Smith
Photographers  Sian Irvine and Karl Adamson

Visit our website at www.davidandcharles.co.uk

David & Charles books are available from all good bookshops; alternatively you can contact our Orderline on 0870 9908222 or write to us at FREEPOST EX2 110, D&C Direct, Newton Abbot, TQ12 4ZZ (no stamp required UK only); US customers call 800-289-0963 and Canadian customers call 800-840-5220.

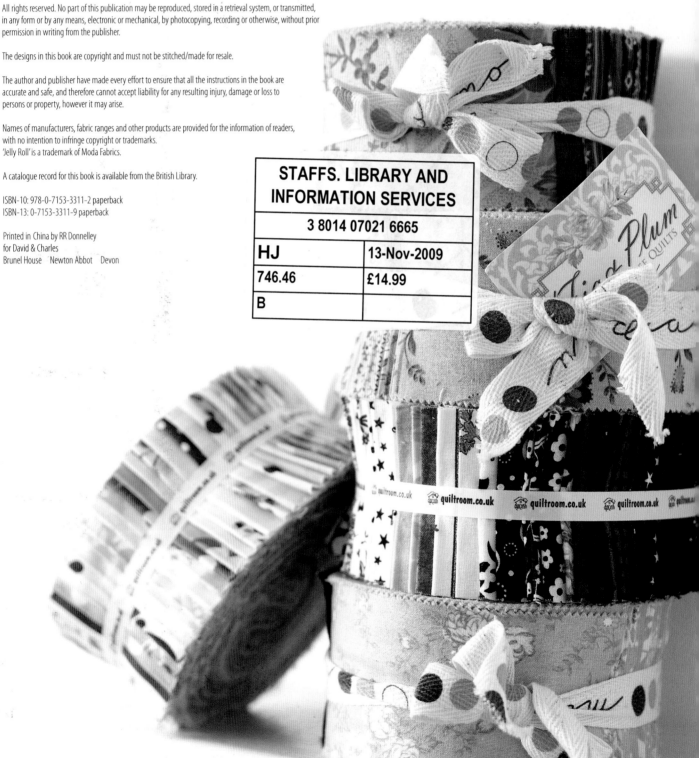

# Contents

**Hidden in the Stars**
10

**Peace Medallion**
42

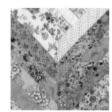

**Candy Heart**
72

**Pick and Mix**
18

**Beach Hut Parade**
50

**Zen and the Jelly Roll**
80

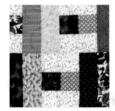

**Vertical Drop**
26

**Birthday Gift**
58

**Jelly Roll Bargello**
88

**May Flowers**
34

**Knickerbocker Glory**
66

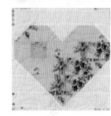

**Be My Valentine**
96

**Valentine Cushion**
108

# Introduction

We knew there was an astounding array of talent out there and the Jelly Roll Challenge was set to find out exactly where it was!

The criteria for the quilts was not that they had to be complex or difficult to make but that they had to make good use of the jelly roll fabrics in a design that would inspire others. Choosing the winning quilts was extremely difficult and we hope we have chosen designs that will inspire you to 'have a go' and unravel those beautifully packaged strips of fabric which we have come to love. The quilt designs certainly inspired us.

The winning quilt featured on the front cover of this book, Be My Valentine, is a great quilt and a worthy winner. It is challenging – but we did call it a jelly roll 'challenge'! You will find the quilt on page 96, so if you do not feel ready for it yet, you can progress through the book trying all the other superb designs first. Templates are used to make the quilt – cleverly placed on the jelly roll to make the most of every inch of fabric. We have, however, given a cushion variation which enables the shapes to be cut using an Omnigrid 96 ruler instead of templates. We do like to give you every option!

We have placed the quilts through the book in what we feel is the order of difficulty and certainly not in the placement of the competition. Thanks to everyone who took part in the Challenge – you have given us so much pleasure. The standard of the entries was very high and congratulations to the quilters whose quilts are included here. You should be feeling very proud of yourselves.

At the end of each chapter there is a variation of each quilt made by us, showing how the design might look with a different choice of fabrics. We had great fun making these variations – now it is your turn. Choose a pattern to try, and then another, and another and enjoy them as much as we did.

Pam and Nicky

Here are the three gorgeous winning quilts of the Jelly Roll Challenge competition – Be My Valentine, Beach Hut Parade and Birthday Gift – showing just how versatile jelly rolls are, and how wonderful inventive quilters are.

# Getting Started

## What is a Jelly Roll?

A jelly roll is a roll of forty fabrics cut in 2½in wide strips across the width of the fabric. All patterns assumed that fabric will be at least 42in wide. Moda introduced jelly rolls to showcase new fabric ranges. How inspirational to have one 2½in wide strip of each new fabric wrapped up so deliciously! Our thanks go to Moda for inspiring us and allowing us to use the name jelly roll in this book.

If you want to make any of the quilts in this book and don't have a jelly roll to use, then cut a 2½in wide strip from forty fabrics from your stash.

We know jelly rolls look so gorgeous you don't like to unroll them – they are an art form in themselves – however they make great quilts too!

So go on – untie the ribbon and be inspired by forty different coordinating fabrics. Just flick through these pages and see the quilts you can make with *just one roll*! Be inspired by the makers of these quilts who did just that.

## Imperial or Metric?

Jelly rolls from Moda are cut 2½in wide and at The Quilt Room we have continued to cut our strip bundles 2½in wide. When quilt making, it is impossible to mix metric and imperial measurements. It would be absurd to have a 2½in strip and tell you to cut it 6cm to make a square! It wouldn't be square and nothing would fit. This caused a dilemma when writing instructions for these quilts and a decision had to be made. All the instructions therefore are written in inches. To convert inches to centimetres, multiply the inch measurement by 2.54. For your convenience fabric requirements are given in both metric and imperial.

## Seam Allowance

We cannot stress enough the importance of maintaining an accurate scant ¼in (6mm) seam allowance throughout. Please take the time to check your seam allowance with the quick test on page 114.

## Quilt Size

In this book the quilts show what can be achieved with just one jelly roll. For the competition, additional fabric of up to 3 yards could be added to the jelly roll but the basis of each quilt is just one jelly roll. If you want to make a larger version of any quilt please refer to the vital statistics at the beginning of all the quilt instructions and these details will help you calculate your requirements.

## Diagrams

Diagrams have been provided to assist you in making the quilts and these are normally beneath or beside the relevant stepped instruction. The direction in which fabric should be pressed in is indicated by arrows on the diagrams. The reverse side of the fabric is shown in a lighter colour than the right side.

## Washing Notes

It is important that pre-cut strips are **not** washed before use. Save the washing until your quilt is complete and then make use of a colour catcher in the wash or possibly dry clean the quilt.

# Hidden in the Stars

## Designed by Sarah Soward

### VITAL STATISTICS

| | |
|---|---|
| Quilt size: | 54in x 62in |
| Block size: | 10in x 6in |
| Number of blocks: | 35 |
| Setting: | 7 x 5 blocks with 2in inner, middle and outer borders |

"I love jelly rolls! I find that quilting with them does so much to ease the stresses of the working day. So far, I have created four jelly roll quilts and one jelly roll and layer cake quilt. When I was told about the competition, I decided that I should produce a design that is fairly simple and not too complicated to make for people who have never used a jelly roll before. I came up with the name 'Hidden in the Stars' for my quilt as the angles that I have cut the jelly roll into make a variation on a star. I hope that you get the same amount of relaxing enjoyment out of creating your own jelly roll quilts as I have done." Sarah Soward

Pam and Nicky's variation quilt on page 17 uses whites, blacks and reds in a dramatic colour combination.

### REQUIREMENTS

- One jelly roll **OR** forty 2½in strips cut across the width of the fabric
- 1½yd (1.5m) of accent fabric for block corners and inner border
- 20in (50cm) of fabric for binding

## Sorting the Jelly Roll Strips

- Choose twenty-seven strips for the blocks. The remaining thirteen strips will be used for your middle and outer borders.
- Read all of the instructions through before starting your quilt. Use a scant ¼in seam allowance throughout.

## Cutting Instructions

### Jelly roll strips:
- Take the thirteen strips allocated for the borders and cut them in half (2½in x 22in).

### Accent fabric:
- Cut seven strips 4¼in wide across the width of the fabric. These are for your block corners.
- Cut seven strips 2½in wide across the width of the fabric. This is for your inner border.

### Binding:
- Cut six 2½in wide strips across the width of the fabric.

## Making the Strip Blocks

**1** From your twenty-seven strips, choose three and sew together along the length to form a set as shown in the diagram below. Repeat with the remaining strips. You need a total of nine sets. To help avoid bowing of the strips, set and press seams before sewing the next strip. Press towards the darker fabric.

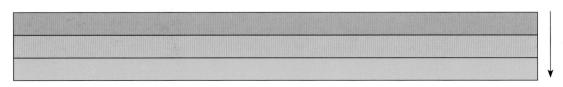

**2** Trim the selvedge and cut four 10½in segments from each set. Straighten the edges between each cut, if necessary. You need thirty-five 10½in sections in total so you will have one spare.

| 10½in | 10½in | 10½in | 10½in |

**3** Position the 60 degree marking on your ruler along one edge as shown below and cut one 60 degree angle from each 10½in section.

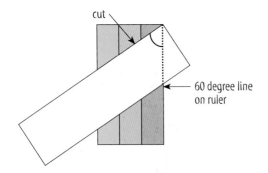

cut

60 degree line
on ruler

**4** Once you have cut the 60 degree angle from each section, attach the sections to the 4¼in strips from your accent fabric. This is done by what is known as the 'washing line' method. You will be able to get five of your sections onto each strip. With your 4¼in strip underneath sew the sections right sides together.

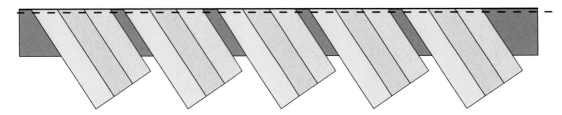

**5** Set the seam and then press seams to your background fabric. Now cut in between each section to separate them.

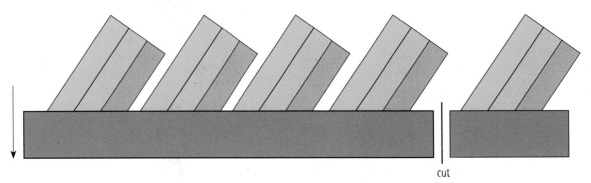

cut

**6** Trim the edges of the background fabric in line with your strip set. Then cut the top off ¼in from the point of the block.

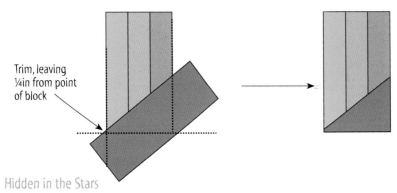

Trim, leaving
¼in from point
of block

## Assembling the Quilt

- Lay out the blocks with seven blocks across and five down, rotating alternate blocks 180 degrees as shown in the diagram below. Sew the blocks together to complete a row.
- Now sew the rows together, pinning at every seam intersection to ensure a perfect match.

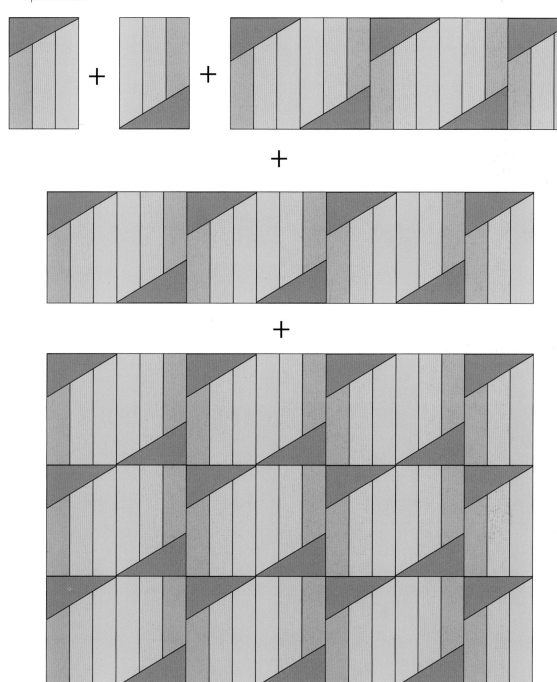

## Adding the Borders

### Inner Border:

- Sew the inner border strips into one continuous length. Measure the vertical length of the quilt top, taking the measurement from the middle of your quilt and cut two lengths to this measurement from your continuous length of inner border fabric. Pin to the sides of your quilt and sew together. Then measure across the horizontal of your quilt top and cut two lengths to this measurement and sew to the top and bottom of your quilt.

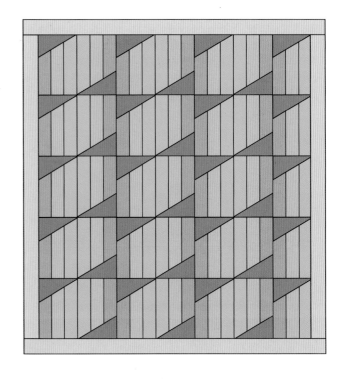

### Middle and outer borders:

- Take the twenty-six jelly roll half strips and sew together to form one continuous length. Add the middle and outer borders, following the instructions for the inner border, above.

## TIP

**When sewing the jelly roll half strips for her middle and outer borders, Sarah sewed them on the diagonal to create added interest. If you wish to do the same, refer to Joining Borders and Binding Strips on page 118.**

## Finishing the Quilt

Your quilt top is now complete. Prepare the top for quilting and then quilt as desired. Bind the quilt to finish (see page 120).

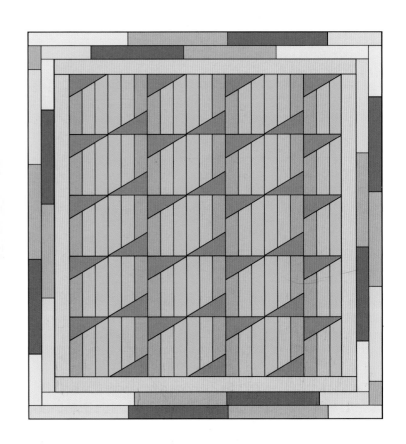

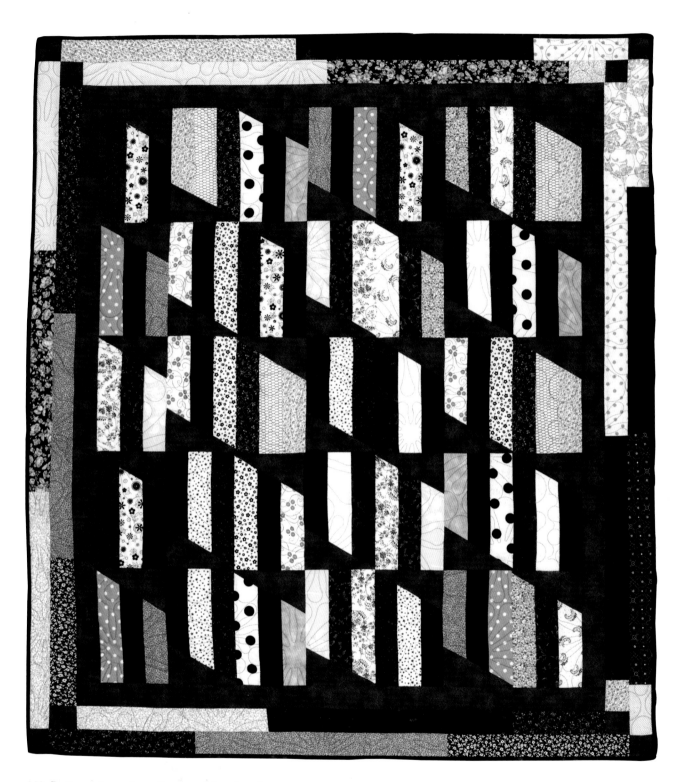

# Hidden in the Stars Variation

We chose to make our variation in a black and white jelly roll with a red accent fabric. This is a perfect example of how to create a stunning quilt in the simplest way possible. The large blocks are quick and easy to piece and the quilt goes together in no time at all. It would be a good quilt to inspire a budding quilter. We need to encourage the next generation to start quilting and this quilt might be the perfect opportunity. In our variation, we added cornerstones from our excess accent fabric to add an extra dimension to the borders. Quilt made by Pam and Nicky Lintott and longarm quilted by The Quilt Room.

# Pick and Mix

## Designed by Angela Davies

### VITAL STATISTICS
Quilt size:        58in x 85in
Block size:        8in square
Number of blocks:  39

"I have always had a love of fabric and sewing from an early age and was taught much by my Gran, who was a good needlewoman. I was inspired to make this quilt when I bought a jelly roll of Thirties reproduction fabrics at a quilt show. I have always loved these fabrics and couldn't wait to get started. I wanted to make a quilt that had different coloured blocks and I tied the theme of the quilt together by having the same white fabric border around all of the blocks. I think the final result is a really pretty quilt." Angela Davies

Pam and Nicky's variation quilt on page 25 also uses a mix of reproduction fabrics but in this instance they were reproduction fabrics from the American Civil War.

### REQUIREMENTS

- One jelly roll **OR** forty 2½in strips cut across the width of the fabric
- 1¼yd (1.25m) of background fabric
- Fat quarter of five coordinating fabrics for setting triangles
- 24in (60cm) fabric for binding (or offcuts and the balance of the fat quarters could be used)

## Sorting the Jelly Roll Strips
- Pair up the strips. Each pair of strips will make two blocks.
- Read all of the instructions through before starting your quilt. Use a scant ¼in seam allowance throughout.

## Cutting Instructions
### Jelly roll strips:
- From each strip cut the following.
  Two 2½in squares.
  Two 2½in x 4½in rectangles.
  One 2½in x 6½in rectangle.
  Two 2½in x 7in rectangles. Set these aside for the border.
  The remaining offcuts can be set aside for the binding.

### Background fabric:
- Cut seventeen strips 2½in wide across the width of the fabric.
- Take seven strips and subcut each strip into six rectangles each 2½in x 6½in.
- Take ten strips and subcut each strip into four rectangles 2½in x 8½in.

### Setting triangles:
- From four of the five fat quarters cut one 12½in square. Cut across both diagonals of each square as shown below to form sixteen setting triangles.

- From the remaining fat quarter cut two 6½in squares. Cut across the diagonal to form the four corner triangles. Cutting the setting triangles and corner triangles in this way ensures that the outer edges of your quilt are not on the bias.

### Binding:
- Cut your binding fabric into eight 2½in wide strips across the width of the fabric.

## Sewing the Blocks
**1** Take one pair of cut strips, allocating one to be fabric A and the other fabric B. With right sides together, sew a fabric A 2½in square to a fabric B 2½in square.

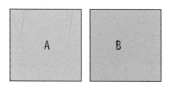

**2** Take a fabric B 2½in x 4½in rectangle and with right sides together sew it to the bottom of the AB unit.

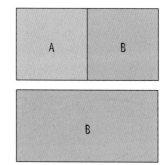

**3** Take a fabric A 2½in x 4½in rectangle and with right sides together sew it to the right-hand side of the unit.

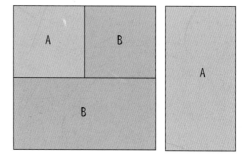

**4** Take a fabric A 2½in x 6½in rectangle and with right sides together sew it to the bottom of the unit.

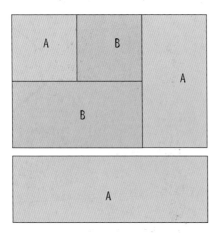

**5** Take a background rectangle 2½in x 6½in and with right sides together sew it to the right-hand side of the unit.

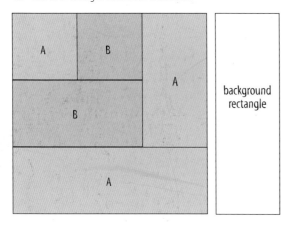

background rectangle

**6** Take a background rectangle 2½in x 8½in and with right sides together sew it to the bottom of the unit.

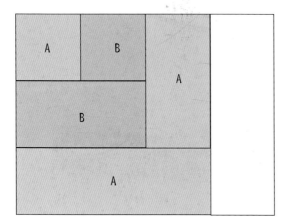

background rectangle

**7** Using the remaining pieces from the pair of fabrics A and B make another block with the fabrics in reverse order. Repeat with all twenty pairs of fabric strips until you have forty blocks. You only need thirty-nine so one block will be spare.

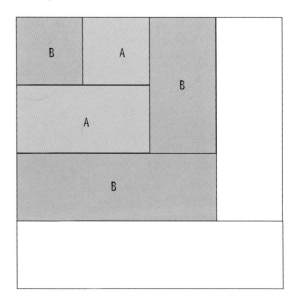

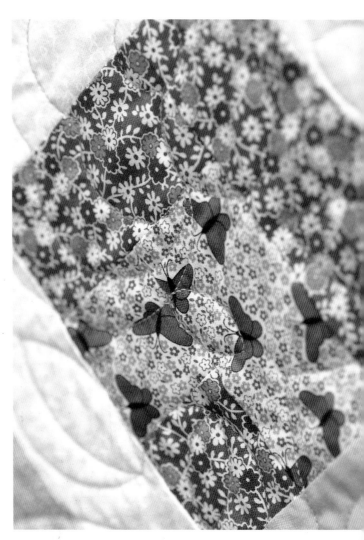

## Assembling the Quilt

- Lay out the blocks and setting triangles and when you are happy with the placement, sew a setting triangle to each side of a block to create row 1 (see Tip, right).
- Following the diagram below, continue to sew the blocks together to form rows with a setting triangle at each end.
- Sew the rows together, pinning at every seam intersection to ensure a perfect match. Sew the four corner triangles on last. Press the work.

# TIP

**The setting triangles are cut a little larger than the block. When sewing these triangles to each side of a block, align the *bottom* of the triangle with the *bottom* of the block.**

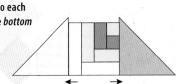

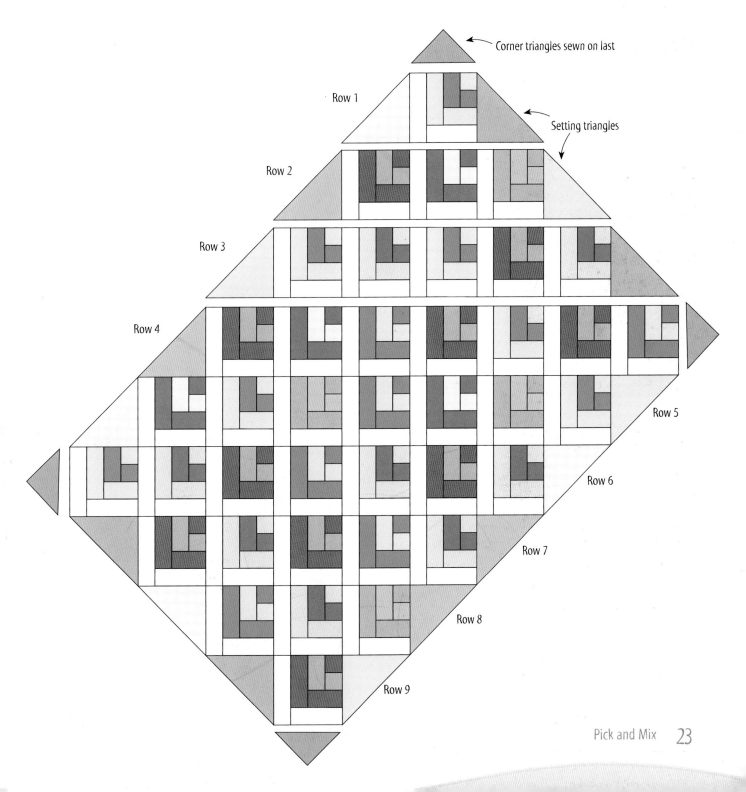

Corner triangles sewn on last

Setting triangles

Row 1

Row 2

Row 3

Row 4

Row 5

Row 6

Row 7

Row 8

Row 9

## Adding the Borders

- Sew the 2½in x 7in rectangles set aside for the borders into one continuous length. Determine the vertical measurement from top to bottom through the centre of your quilt top. Cut two side borders to this measurement. Pin and then sew these borders to the quilt.
- Now determine the horizontal measurement from side to side across the centre of the quilt top. Cut two borders to this measurement. Pin and sew to the quilt.
- Repeat this process with the second border.

## Finishing the Quilt

Your quilt top is now complete. Prepare the top for quilting and then quilt as desired. Bind the quilt to finish (see page 120). If you are using offcuts to bind the quilt you need approximately 300in.

# Pick and Mix Variation >>

It is difficult to improve on Angela's gorgeous Thirties mix of fabrics. We decided to keep to the heritage theme and used an American Civil war reproduction range from Moda's Collection for a Cause – Legacy by Howard Marcus. We loved the way Angela used varied setting triangles in this quilt, which really brought it to life – a tip we will certainly remember. Quilt made by Pam and Nicky Lintott and longarm quilted by The Quilt Room.

# Vertical Drop

## Designed by Shelagh Roberts

### VITAL STATISTICS

Quilt size: 68in x 78in
Block size: 4in x 6in
Number of blocks: 170 + 10 half blocks
Setting: 10 x 17½ blocks plus 4in border

"I started patchworking thirty years ago and have always been interested in simple geometric designs. I made my first jelly roll quilt using a commercially produced roll, which got me hooked. I made this quilt using my stash and decided to have a simple design that used fairly large pieces in order to showcase the fabrics. The smaller squares in the design allow a large number of fabric combinations. I used the same fabric for the border as the background, which allows the design to 'float'. It pieces together easily, with seams butting together neatly. It would be an ideal project for a novice machine quilter." Shelagh Roberts

Pam and Nicky's variation quilt shown on page 33 uses lovely blues and reds on a medium background fabric, which creates quite a different look.

### REQUIREMENTS

- One jelly roll **OR** forty 2½in strips cut across the width of the fabric, twenty dark and twenty light/medium
- 1¾yd (1.6m) of background fabric
- 1yd (1m) of border fabric
- 24in (60cm) of fabric for binding

## Sorting the Jelly Roll Strips

- Sort the strips into twenty darks and twenty light/mediums.
- Read all of the instructions through before starting your quilt. Use a scant ¼in seam allowance throughout.

## Cutting Instructions

### Dark jelly roll strips:

- Take ten strips and cut each one into the following rectangles.
  One 2½in x 33½in.
  One 2½in x 8½in.
- From the remaining ten dark strips cut each one into the following rectangles.
  One 2½in x 27in.
  One 2½in x 16in.

### Light jelly roll strips:

- Cut the light jelly roll strips exactly as you have cut the dark strips.

### Background fabric:

- Cut twenty-four strips 2½in wide across the width of the fabric
- Subcut twenty strips into the following.
  Two 2½in x 16in.
  One 2½in x 8½in.
- Subcut each of the remaining four strips into five rectangles 2½in x 8½in. You will get five to a strip. In total, you need forty 2½in x 16in rectangles and forty 2½in x 8½in rectangles.

### Border fabric:

- Cut eight 4½in strips across the width of the fabric.

### Binding:

- Cut eight 2½in strips across the width of the fabric.

## Sewing the Blocks

**1** Take one dark 33½in strip and one light/medium 33½in strip and with right sides together sew along the long side. Press the seam towards the dark fabric. Cut five 6½in segments from the strip.

**2** Repeat this sewing and cutting process with the other nine pairs of 33½in dark and light/medium strips.

**3** Repeat the process again with the ten 27in dark and light/medium strips. Cut four 6½in segments from each strip. In total you need ninety segments. These form unit A.

Unit A

**4** Take one 8½in strip of dark fabric and two 8½in strips of background fabric. With right sides together, sew a background strip to either side of the dark strip. Press to the dark strip. Cut three 2½in segments from the strip unit. Repeat with the other nine 8½in dark strips.

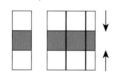

**5** Repeat the process with the 16in strips of dark fabric. You will get six segments from each strip unit. In total you need ninety segments. These form unit B.

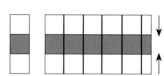

Unit B

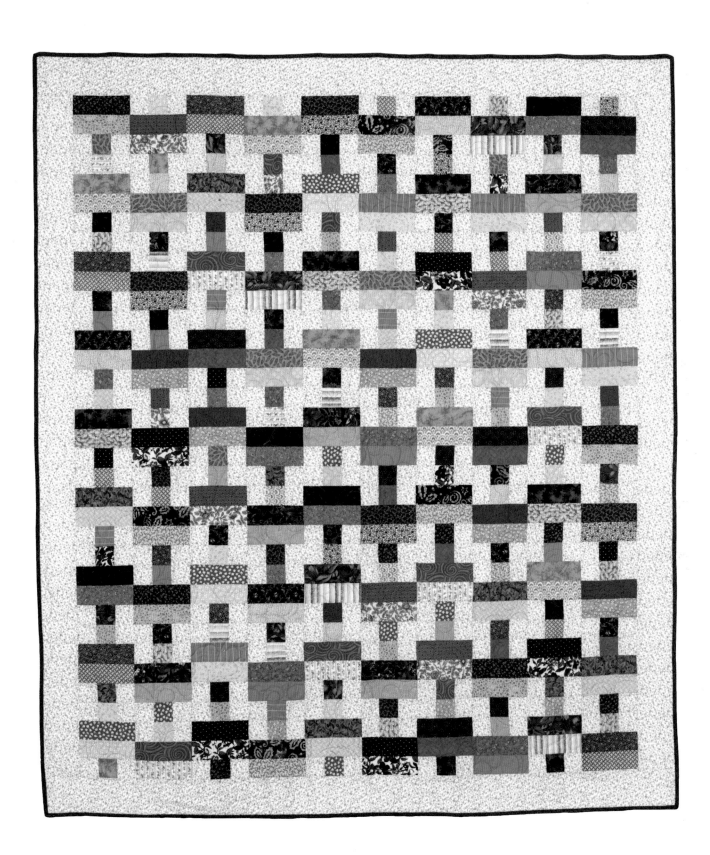

**6** Take one 8½in strip of light/medium fabric and two 8½in strips of background fabric and, with right sides together, sew a background strip to either side of the light/medium strip. Press to the background strips. Pressing the strips in this direction will ensure the seams nest together nicely when they are sewn together. Cut three 2½in segments from the strip unit.

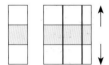

**7** Repeat this cutting and sewing process with the other nine 8½in light/medium strips.

**8** Repeat the process with the ten 16in strips of light/medium fabric. You will get six segments from each strip unit. In total you need ninety segments. These form unit C.

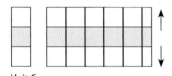

Unit C

**9** Now take a unit B and a unit C and, with right sides together, sew down the long side, pinning at every seam intersection to ensure a perfect match. Press to the dark square. This is unit D. Repeat until you have eighty unit D. You will have twenty segments left. Set ten aside for the half blocks and the other ten are spare.

Unit D

## TIP

**Take good care of your sewing machine and you will be well rewarded. It really does need a little love and attention at times and will respond well to cleaning and removing the lint that accumulates, regular oiling and, most important of all, changing the needle regularly.**

## Assembling the Quilt

- Referring to the diagram below, lay out the blocks alternating unit A and unit D in vertical columns. The first column contains nine unit A alternating with eight unit D ending with a half block. The second column starts with a half block followed by nine unit A and eight unit D. Continue for ten columns. When you are happy with the layout sew the blocks into columns, pinning at every seam intersection to ensure a perfect match.
- Press the seams of each column in the opposite direction before sewing the columns together so they nest together nicely when sewn. Press the work.

# TIP

Keep a stack of little scraps of fabric beside your sewing machine and always use one to finish a row of sewing, keeping it under the machine foot until you are ready to start sewing again. There is then no need to waste thread when starting to sew by holding on to the ends, as you are all ready to go. Most importantly, you don't have to spend hours snipping threads off your quilt, as the thread ends remain on your fabric scraps. We do encourage you to get into this habit as it is a thread saver and time saver.

half block

half block

## Adding the Borders

- Join the 4½in border strips together to form a continuous length. Determine the vertical measurement from top to bottom through the centre of your quilt top. Cut two side borders to this measurement. Pin and sew to the quilt, easing if necessary.
- Now determine the horizontal measurement from side to side across the centre of the quilt top. Cut two borders to this measurement. Pin and sew to the quilt. Press to the border fabric.

## Finishing the Quilt

Your quilt top is now complete. Prepare the top for quilting and then quilt as desired. Bind the quilt to finish (see page 120).

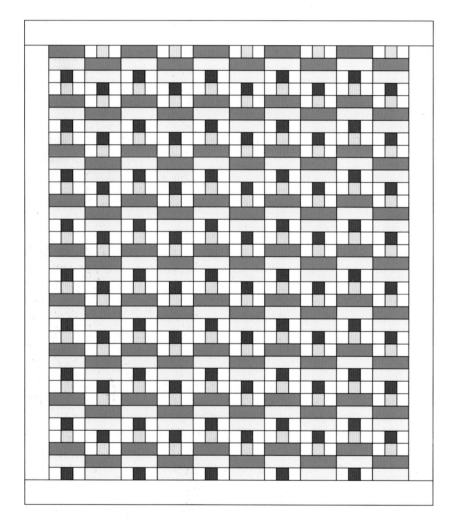

## Vertical Drop Variation >>

In our variation we decided to have a medium background instead of a light one to see how it would look. Our jelly roll is Portobello Market from Moda, which has a lovely selection of blues and reds, and we chose a tone on tone blue also from Moda. We really liked the effect and it is interesting to see the importance of the background fabric to create the effect you want from your quilt. Quilt made by Pam and Nicky Lintott and longarm quilted by The Quilt Room.

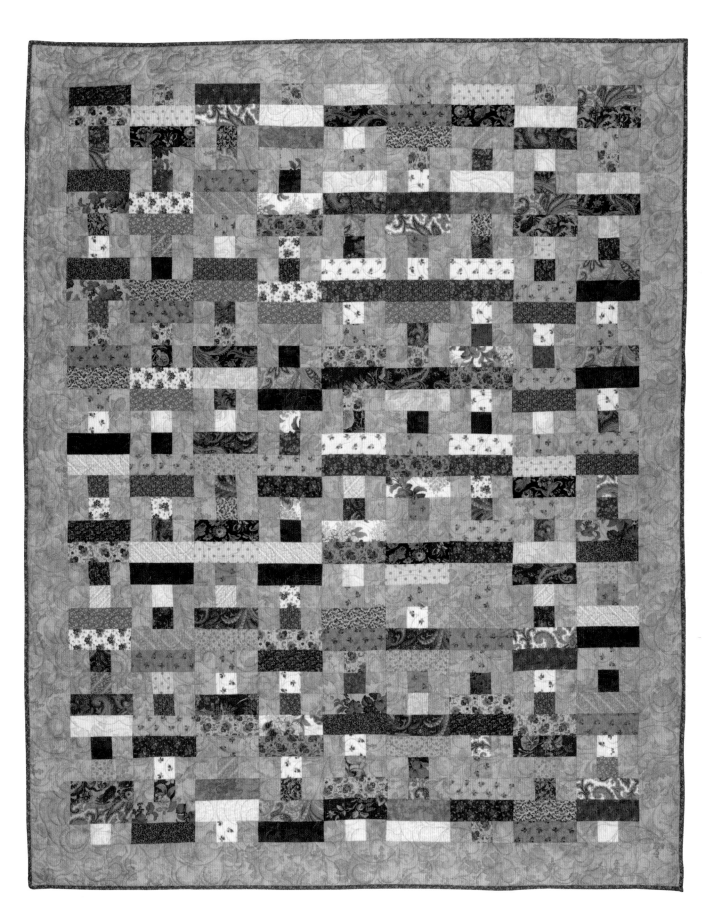

# May Flowers

## Designed by Joanne Ridley

### VITAL STATISTICS

| | |
|---|---|
| Quilt size: | 61in x 81in |
| Block size: | 10in square |
| Number of blocks: | 35 |
| Setting: | 5 x 7 blocks plus ¾in and 4¾in borders |

"I love designing simple but effective quilts and it's great to create something that looks stunning but is quick to produce and isn't scary to piece. For this quilt for the competition I decided to combine quilting and appliqué and chose a jelly roll that was vibrant and summery and complemented the flower design. The flowers can be appliquéd in any way you fancy – using fusible webbing is easy and the edges of the flowers can be left ragged or concealed with a fine blanket stitch. I made good use of the jelly roll, with only one and a half strips unused. An additional 2¼yd of fabric was needed to produce this useful sized quilt, which I long arm quilted myself." Joanne Ridley

Pam and Nicky's variation quilt on page 41 uses an attractive blue and white fabric combination, which gives this pretty design a very fresh look.

### REQUIREMENTS

- One jelly roll **OR** forty 2½in (6.3cm) strips cut across the width of the fabric
- 2½yd (2.25m) of fabric for background and outer border
- 24in (60cm) of fabric for binding

## Sorting the Jelly Roll Strips

- Choose twenty-three strips for the pieced blocks.
- Choose twelve strips for the appliqué blocks.
- Choose four strips for the inner border. There will be one spare strip – you might need it if you have a piecing disaster!
- Read all of the instructions through before starting your quilt. Use a scant ¼in seam allowance throughout.

Background fabric pieces

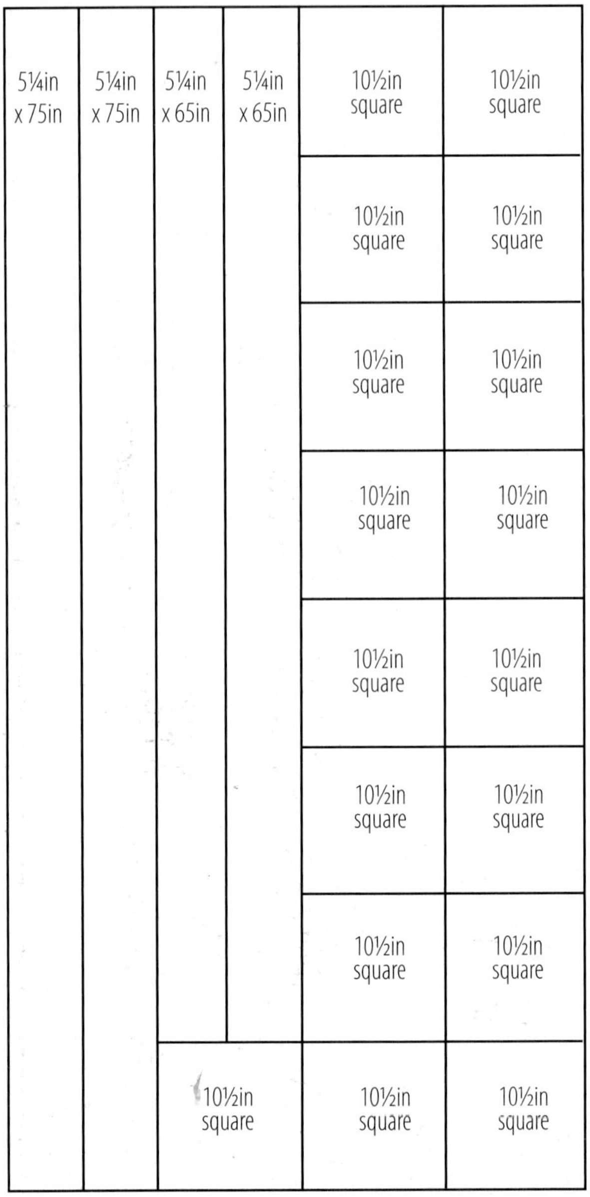

| 5¼in x 75in | 5¼in x 75in | 5¼in x 65in | 5¼in x 65in | 10½in square | 10½in square |
|---|---|---|---|---|---|
| | | | | 10½in square | 10½in square |
| | | | | 10½in square | 10½in square |
| | | | | 10½in square | 10½in square |
| | | | | 10½in square | 10½in square |
| | | | | 10½in square | 10½in square |
| | | | | 10½in square | 10½in square |
| | | 10½in square | | 10½in square | 10½in square |

## Cutting Instructions

### Pieced blocks:

- Cut each of the twenty-three strips into four rectangles 2½in x 10½in. You need ninety rectangles and will have two spare.

### Inner border:

- Take the four strips allocated for the inner border and cut each one in half lengthways to yield eight strips 1¼in wide by the width of the fabric.

### Background fabric:

- First cut the border strips from the length of the fabric. You need two side borders cut 5¼in x 75in and two borders for the top and bottom cut 5¼in x 65in – see diagram, left. Note: these lengths are oversized to allow for accurate measuring and trimming when you add your borders.
- From the remaining fabric cut seventeen squares 10½in x 10½in for the appliqué blocks.

### Binding:

- Cut your fabric into eight 2½in wide strips across the width of the fabric.

## Sewing the Striped Blocks

Sort the 10½in strips into sets of five. Sew the five strips together, alternating the sewing directions to avoid warping. Press all seams to one side. Sew eighteen blocks in this way.

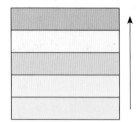

## Sewing the Appliqué Blocks

**1** Sort the twelve strips into three sets of four. Sew each set of four strips together, alternating the direction of sewing as before to avoid warping the strip unit. Press all seams open to make it less bulky when you appliqué the final flower shape on to the background. Label your three strip units A, B and C.

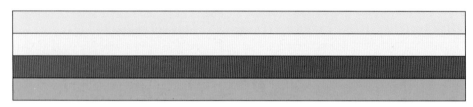

**2** From each strip unit cut two 3½in segments and five 7in segments as shown in the diagram below.

| 3½in | 7in | 7in | 7in | 7in | 7in | 3½in |

**3** Re-sew the segments back into three sets, alternating the segments from the three A, B and C sets as you do so (see diagram below). Doing this will result in a good mixture of colours and fabrics in each appliqué flower. Press all seams open.

| A | B | C | A | B | C | A |
|---|---|---|---|---|---|---|
| 3½in | 7in | 7in | 7in | 7in | 7in | 3½in |

| B | C | A | B | C | A | B |
|---|---|---|---|---|---|---|
| 3½in | 7in | 7in | 7in | 7in | 7in | 3½in |

| C | A | B | C | A | B | C |
|---|---|---|---|---|---|---|
| 3½in | 7in | 7in | 7in | 7in | 7in | 3½in |

**4** Lay out six flower shapes on two strip sets, as shown in the diagram below, and five on the third strip set. You need seventeen in total. Position the template centrally on a vertical seamline in the strip set each time and rotate the template from flower to flower so that the seamlines are in different places on each flower to give more variation and interest to the finished quilt. There is very little wastage so lay out your shapes on the strip set to ensure they all fit on before cutting. Cut out the flower shapes.

**5** Now use your preferred method of appliqué to attach the flowers. (See page 117 for advice on appliqué.)

### If using raw edge appliqué:
Joanne's quilt used this method. Cut out the flowers using pinking shears. After positioning a flower in the centre of the background square, pin it in place and pin a removable stabilizer to the reverse of the background square. Sew a line of machine running stitches inside the edge all the way round.

### If using fusible web appliqué:
The variation quilt used this method. Draw around the template seventeen times on to the paper side of the fusible web and then iron the shapes on to the reverse of the strip sets. Cut out on the line and fuse in place in the centre of each of the 10½in background squares, making sure you are happy with the orientation of the flower.

**6** To ensure that the rest of the flower blocks match the orientation of the first block, lay out the completed first block and place a background square on top of it. Looking through the background square it is now possible to position the flower in the right place on the second and subsequent blocks. If you can't see through your background fabric, use a light box or tape the first block to a sunny window.

**7** When all the appliqué is complete remove the stabilizer, if used, and press the blocks on the reverse.

## TIP
**Place a pin on the top edge of every block so that when sewing the blocks into rows you can easily make sure that all the flowers are the same way up.**

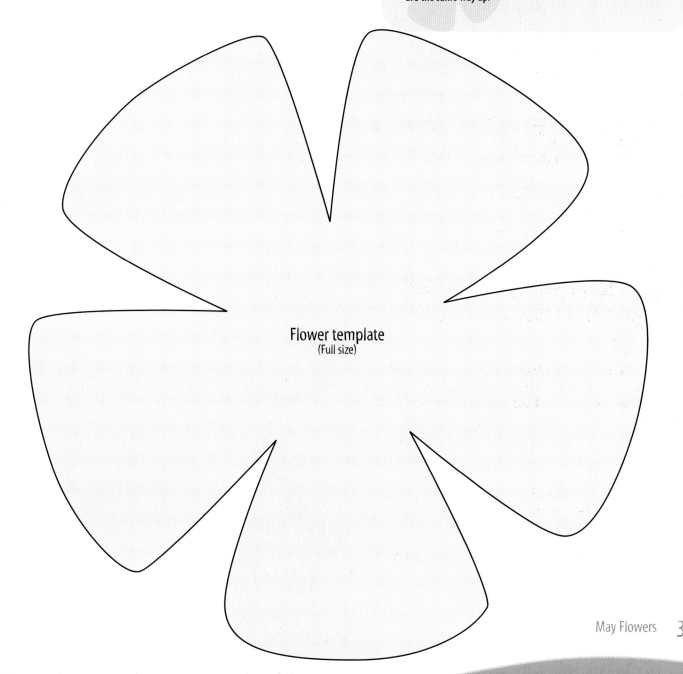

Flower template
(Full size)

## Assembling the Quilt

- Lay out your blocks and when you are happy with the placement, sew the blocks together into seven rows of five blocks, pressing towards the appliqué blocks each time.
- Now sew the rows together, pressing the seams to one side.

## Adding the Borders

- Sew the eight 1¼in strips together into one continuous strip. Measure your quilt top through the centre, top to bottom, and cut two strips to this length. Sew these strips to the sides of the quilt and press the seams towards the borders.
- Now measure your quilt top through the centre from side to side. Cut two strips to this measurement and sew to the top and bottom of the quilt. Press seams towards the borders.
- Repeat with the outer border strips, trimming them to the exact measurements of your quilt. Sew on the side borders first, pressing to the borders, and then sew on the top and bottom borders.

## Finishing the Quilt

Your quilt top is now complete. Prepare the top for quilting and then quilt as desired. Bind the quilt to finish (see page 120).

## May Flowers Variation >>

We love blue and white quilts and we couldn't resist trying this pattern out in a blue jelly roll with a white background. We hope you like the effect as much as we do. As an alternative to frayed edge appliqué, this quilt is made using fusible webbing and the edges were secured with an invisible machine stitch. Many alternatives could be used here – possibly making a feature of a blanket stitch around the edges. The quilt was made by Pam and Nicky Lintott with appliqué blocks made by Gwen Jones and longarm quilted by The Quilt Room.

# Peace Medallion

## Designed by Paula Diggle

### VITAL STATISTICS

| | |
|---|---|
| Quilt size: | 60in x 48in |
| Block size: | 6in square |
| Number of blocks: | 48 |
| Setting: | 6 x 8 plus 2in plain borders and 2in pieced border |

"This impressive quilt isn't hard to make. It uses just one easy block and when you have completed the blocks the quilt top comes together quickly and easily, with the pattern growing in a most rewarding way. The design needs a jelly roll with at least three different main colourways, but most jelly rolls have more than that. The one I used was Peace on Earth (Three Sisters for Moda), which has five main colourways, so I had fun choosing which colourway should go in which area of the design. The jelly roll fabrics have quite distinctive patterning so it seemed a good idea to calm the design down with plain, simple borders." Paula Diggle

Pam and Nicky's variation quilt on page 49 uses a lovely pastel range of fabrics to create a softer effect.

### REQUIREMENTS

- One jelly roll **OR** forty 2½in strips cut across the width of the fabric
- 1yd (1m) of border fabric
- 20in (50cm) of binding fabric
- Omnigrid 96 ruler

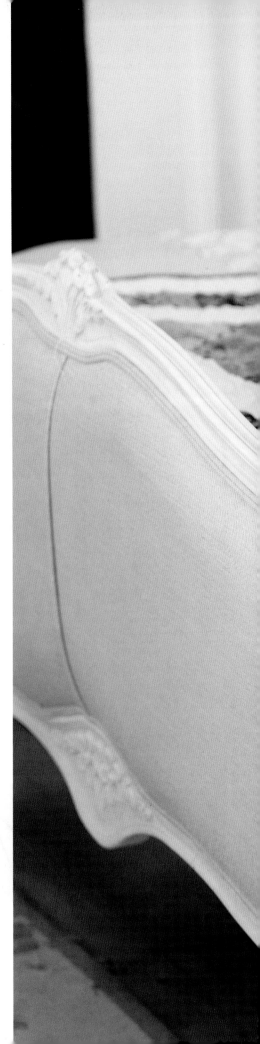

## Sorting the Jelly Roll Strips

- The quilt needs at least three different main colourways. Be guided by the colour mix you have in your chosen jelly roll. The Peace on Earth jelly roll used in this quilt had five colourways divided as follows (see diagram right).
  Three strips of colour A (brown).
  Seven strips of colour B (blue).
  Eleven strips of colour C (cream).
  Seven strips of colour D (red).
  Four strips of colour E (green).
  Two strips of colour F (blue).
  Two strips of colour G (green).
- You have four spare strips that will be needed for the pieced border and can also be used in the quilt to give variety in the blocks.
- Read all of the instructions through before starting your quilt. Use a scant ¼in seam allowance throughout.

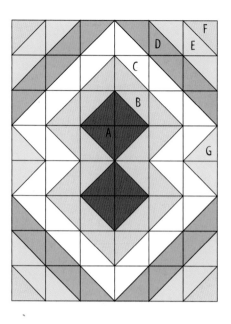

## Basic Block

- The centre of the quilt is composed of forty-eight mock log cabin blocks. Each is made in the same way using three 2½in squares of each colour and three half squares of each colour (see diagram right). The combinations you will need are as follows.
  Colours A and B – 8 blocks.
  Colours B and C – 12 blocks.
  Colours C and D – 12 blocks.
  Colours D and E – 8 blocks.
  Colours E and F – 4 blocks.
  Colours C and G – 4 blocks.

## Cutting Instructions
### Border fabric:
- Cut eleven strips 2½in wide across the width of the fabric. Set five aside for the inner border and six for the outer borders.

### Binding:
- Cut your fabric into seven 2½in wide strips across the width of the fabric.

## Making the A and B blocks

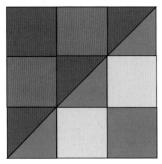

**1** Start by making the half-square triangles as follows. Press one colour A strip and one colour B strip right sides together (see diagram below), ensuring that they are exactly one on top of the other. The pressing will help to hold the two strips together.

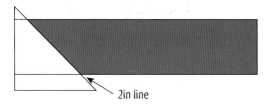

**2** Lay out on the cutting mat and trim the selvedge on the left side. Position the Omnigrid 96 ruler as shown in the diagram below, lining up the 2in mark at the bottom edge of the strips, and cut the first triangle. You will notice that the cut out triangle has a flat top. This would just have been a dog ear you needed to cut off, so is saving you time!

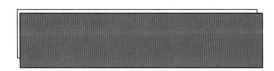

2in line

**3** Rotate the Omnigrid ruler 180 degrees to the right as shown below and cut the next triangle. Continue in this way along the strip. You need twenty-four sets of triangles in total from one strip.

2in line

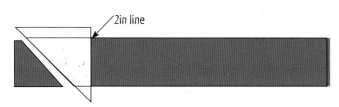

**4** Sew along the diagonals to form twenty-four half-square triangles. Trim all dog ears and press open with seams pressed towards the darker fabric. You need twenty-four half-square triangles from A and B in total.

**5** Subcut the remaining two A strips and B strips into 2½in squares. You will get sixteen from each strip. You need twenty-four of each in total. Set the remaining squares to one side to be used in the border or to give variety in other blocks.

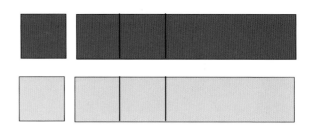

**6** Arrange the blocks as shown in the diagram below, trying not to put the same fabric next to each other. Sew into strips, pressing the seams in the directions indicated. Sew the strips together and the seams will nest together nicely. Make eight blocks in total.

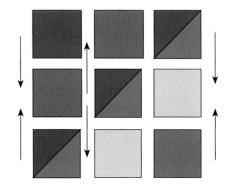

## Making the B and C Blocks

**1** Cut one B strip and one C strip in half so that they measure 2½in x 22in. Then with one and a half B strips and one and a half C strips create thirty-six half-square triangles, following the instructions for the A and B blocks, left. You will get twenty-four half-square triangles from the whole strips and twelve from the half strips. You need thirty-six half-square triangles from B and C in total.

**2** Subcut the remaining two and a half B strips and two and a half C strips into 2½in squares. You will get sixteen from each strip. You need thirty-six of each in total. Set the remaining squares to one side to be used in the border.

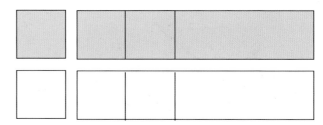

**3** Arrange the blocks as shown below, trying not to put the same fabric next to each other. Sew into strips pressing the seams as before and then sew the strips together. Make twelve blocks in total.

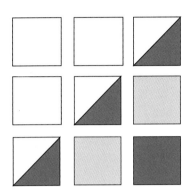

## Making the C and D Blocks

Repeat exactly as you have done with the B and C fabrics using the C and D fabrics. You need twelve blocks from the C and D fabrics in total.

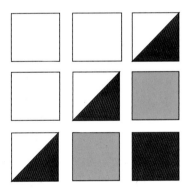

## Making the D and E Blocks

Repeat exactly as you have done with the A and B fabrics using the D and E fabrics. You need eight blocks from the D and E fabrics in total.

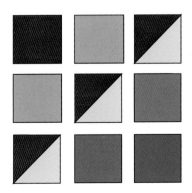

## Making the E and F Blocks

In the same way as before but using your E and F fabrics create four blocks in total.

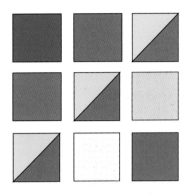

## Making the C and G Blocks

In the same way as before but using your C and G fabrics create four blocks in total.

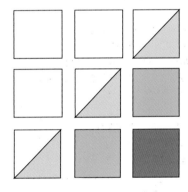

# TIP

**A light grey thread is really all you need for sewing your patchwork together as it blends well with all colours. To save time, pre-wind as many bobbins as you can so you can just pop one in when you need to.**

## Assembling the Quilt

- Referring to the diagram below, arrange your forty-eight blocks into the pattern, finding an arrangement that pleases the eye. Try to achieve a random effect as far as you can, but don't worry if a few similar fabrics end up next to each other. Sew the blocks together in rows and then sew the rows together. The completed centre should measure approximately 36½in x 48½in.

## Adding the Borders

### First border:

- Join five border strips into one continuous length. Determine the vertical measurement from top to bottom through the centre of your quilt top. Cut two side borders to this measurement and sew them to the quilt.
- Now determine the horizontal measurement from side to side across the centre of the quilt top. Cut these two borders to this measurement and sew to the quilt.

### Second border:

- This is made from 2½in squares so gather all your unused 2½in squares and cut more from your unused jelly roll strips. You need two lengths of twenty-six squares and two lengths of twenty-two squares. Sew the lengths of twenty-six squares to the sides and then the lengths of twenty-two squares to the top and bottom.

### Third border:

- Join six border strips into one continuous length following the instructions for adding the first border. Sew to your quilt.

## Finishing the Quilt

Your quilt top is now complete. Prepare the top for quilting and then quilt as desired. Bind the quilt to finish (see page 120).

## Peace Medallion Variation >>

This quilt is a classic example of why we use jelly rolls. It is made from such a simple block but because the fabrics all coordinate beautifully they create a stunning quilt. We just loved the range of fabrics chosen by Paula and decided to make our variation using the Three Sisters range called Aviary. With its pastel pinks and blues it created a lovely quilt – just perfect for a new arrival! Quilt made by Pam and Nicky Lintott and longarm quilted by The Quilt Room.

# Beach Hut Parade

## Designed by Jenny Hutchison

### VITAL STATISTICS

| | |
|---|---|
| Quilt size: | 48in x 64in |
| Block size: | 8in x 12in |
| Number of blocks: | 16 |
| Setting: | 4 x 5 blocks + two 2in borders and a 4in striped |

"I've been making quilts since I was six and find inspiration in many places. When I initially thought about this quilt I envisioned a house block, as I felt that jelly roll strips would be ideal for a design based on rows of houses. Having drawn the design out on squared paper, I saw that the house part of the block would work well using both horizontal and vertical strips, which was when I came up with the idea of beach huts. The colours of the huts were inspired by stripy beehives that I saw in Crete. The fabrics used for the quilt are from the Strawberry Fayre Mediterranean range. Mixing and matching the colourful strips gave me hours of creative fun and I hope you get the same amount of enjoyment out of this quilt design as I did."Jenny Hutchison

For their variation on page 57 Pam and Nicky chose a very different range of fabrics for the beach huts and a blue spotted fabric for the sky, which created a beautifully subtle quilt.

### REQUIREMENTS

- One jelly roll **OR** forty 2½in strips cut across the width of the fabric
- 20in (50cm) of blue sky fabric (if you can use some of your jelly roll strips as sky you will need less extra sky fabric)
- Four 4½in squares for corner blocks from your scrap bag
- 12in (30cm) of fabric for inner borders
- 20in (50cm) of fabric for outer borders
- Binding from jelly roll strips

## Sorting the Jelly Roll Strips

- Sort your strips as follows.
  Sixteen strips for the beach huts.
  One strip for the window.
  Three strips for the window panels.
  One strip for the corner squares for the inner border.
  Ten strips for the striped border.
  Seven strips for the binding.
- Read all of the instructions through before starting your quilt.
  Use a scant ¼in seam allowance throughout.

## Cutting Instructions

### Jelly roll strips:

- From each of your sixteen strips allocated for the beach huts cut the following.
  One rectangle 2½in x 8½in for the roof.
  One rectangle 2½in x 4½in for the roof.
  Two rectangles 2½in x 8½in for the outer beach hut panels.
  One rectangle 2½in x 4½in for the inner beach hut panel.
- From the one strip allocated for the window cut sixteen squares 2½in x 2½in.
- From the three strips allocated for the window panels cut each strip into six squares 2½in x 2½in and six rectangles 2½in x 4½in.
- From the strip allocated for the corner squares cut four squares 2½in x 2½in.

### Sky fabric:

- Cut six 2½in strips across the width of the fabric. Take four strips and subcut each into nine rectangles 2½in x 4½in. You need thirty-two in total.
- Take two strips and subcut each into sixteen squares 2½in x 2½in. You need thirty-two in total.

### Border fabric:

- Cut four 2½in strips across the width of the fabric for the inner border.
- Cut six 2½in strips across the width of the fabric for the outer border.

## Sewing the Beach Hut Sections

**1** Take a 2½in square window panel and a 2½in x 4½in window panel of the same fabric and sew to either side of a window – see diagram below. Press the seams of the window unit in one direction as shown by the arrow on the diagram.

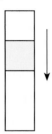

**2** Take a 2½in x 8½in inner beach hut panel and sew to one side of the window unit. Press towards the inner panel. Sew half of the inner panels to the left side of the window unit and the other half to the right.

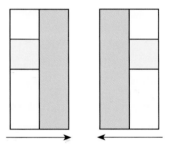

**3** Take two 2½in x 8½in outer beach hut panels of the same fabric and sew to either side. Press seams in one direction.

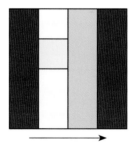

## Sewing the Roof Sections
### Top section:

**1** With right sides together, place one 2½in x 4½in sky section at right angles to one 2½in x 4½in roof section. Using a ruler, draw the diagonal line as shown and sew along this line – see Tip, right. Press open towards the sky fabric and trim away the excess fabric.

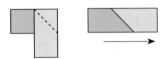

**2** Sew the other 2½in x 4½in sky section in the same way. Press open and trim excess fabric.

### Bottom section:

**3** With right sides together, place a 2½in sky square on the left-hand side of a 2½in x 8½in roof section. Draw a diagonal line and then sew on the line. Press open towards the sky fabric and trim the excess fabric.

**4** Now repeat this procedure on the other side to create the other sky triangle.

**5** With right sides together, join the roof sections, pinning at the seam intersection to ensure a perfect match. Press the work.

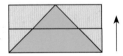

**6** With right sides together, sew the roof section to the hut section to complete the beach hut. For variation you can rotate some of the beach hut sections 90 degrees. Repeat to make sixteen beach huts in total.

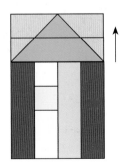

# TIP
When stitching 'flip and sew' corners, instead of sewing exactly on the diagonal line, stitch a thread width to the right of the line and you will find that when you flip the corner back and press it will fit exactly. When sewing exactly on the line, the thickness of the thread can cause the flip and sew corner to be fractionally too small.

## Assembling the Blocks
Lay out the blocks into four rows of four and when you are happy with the arrangement, sew the blocks together, pinning at every seam intersection.

## Piecing the Striped Border

**1** Sew five strips together lengthwise. Press seams in one direction. Trim the selvedge and subcut into nine 4½in segments. Repeat with the other five strips allocated for the striped border.

**2** Sew all the units together to form one continuous length. Divide into two lengths of twenty-six segments for the side borders and two lengths of eighteen segments for the top and bottom borders, unpicking the seams where necessary.

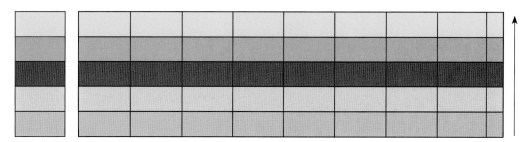

## Adding the Borders

- Join your inner border strips together to form a long length. Determine the vertical measurement from top to bottom of the quilt top. Cut two lengths to this measurement.

- Determine the horizontal measurement from side to side through the centre of the quilt top. Cut two lengths to this measurement plus ½in. Sew the corner squares to both ends of these lengths. Sew the side borders on first and then sew on the top and bottom border, pinning and easing where necessary.

- Pin and sew the side striped borders in place. Sew the 4½in squares to either end of the top and bottom striped border and sew to the quilt, pinning and easing where necessary.

- Join your outer border strips together and sew to your quilt as above.

## Finishing the Quilt

Your quilt top is now complete. Prepare the top for quilting and then quilt as desired. Bind the quilt to finish (see page 120).

## Beach Hut Parade Variation >>

We loved the choice of fabric Jenny used, which evokes memories of blissful summer days by the sea. When choosing our fabric for the variation there was one obvious choice – Beach House from Blackbird Designs – which had lots of striped fabric that we knew would look good. It gave a totally different effect from Jenny's quilt – maybe ours doesn't look quite so sunny – especially as Pam's husband Nick commented that our spotted sky fabric made it look as though it was snowing! The quilt went together very quickly. As we hadn't used any of our jelly roll strips for the sky, we had a few extra strips for the outer border, giving a scrappier effect. Quilt made by Pam and Nicky Lintott and longarm quilted by The Quilt Room.

# Birthday Gift

## Designed by Annie Harris

### VITAL STATISTICS

| | |
|---|---|
| Quilt size: | 60in x 60in |
| Block size: | 16in square |
| Number of blocks: | 9 |
| Setting: | 3 x 3 plus 2in plain border and a 4in pieced border made from cut off jelly roll triangles |

"I first discoved the delights of quilting during the 80s when I moved to England from the tiny village where I was brought up in France.

I joined a class that helped me see the endless design possibilities offered by patchwork and quilting. This quilt was inspired by a very distorted photograph of a quilt I once saw. I looked for the pattern but could not find it anywhere, so ended up working it out for myself. I called the quilt Birthday Gift because I thought the block design resembled the top of a gift-wrapped box. This quilt holds a special place in my heart and I would like to dedicate it to my father's philosophy of looking to the future. I greatly look forward to passing it down through my family to a future grandchild in due course." Annie Harris

Pam and Nicky's variation on page 65 uses a soft and gentle range of fabrics from Fig Tree Quilts, for a very different but effective look.

### REQUIREMENTS

- One jelly roll **OR** forty 2½in strips cut across the width of the fabric
- 2½yd (2.25m) of background fabric
- Offcuts from the jelly roll strips for the binding

## Sorting the Jelly Roll Strips

- Sort the jelly roll strips into ten piles of four strips according to colour. The strips from one pile will be used to make one block. Set aside the lightest pile of four strips to be used to make the inner border.
- Read all of the instructions through before starting your quilt. Use a scant ¼in seam allowance throughout.

## Cutting Instructions

### Background fabric:

- Cut ten strips 2½in wide and subcut nine strips into four rectangles 2½in x 8½in as shown in the diagram below. You need thirty-six in total. This is Unit D. Set aside the remaining 2½in wide strip with the four lightest jelly roll strips to be used in the inner border.

UNIT D

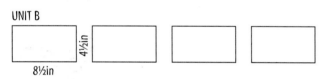

8½in

- Cut nine strips 4½in wide and subcut each strip into four rectangles 4½in x 8½in. You need thirty-six in total. This is unit B.

UNIT B

8½in

- Cut two 5in wide strips and subcut these into ten 5in squares for the outer border.

## Making the Blocks

**1** Working with one pile of four jelly roll strips, take one strip and cut it into four rectangles 2½in x 8½in. This is unit A. Put the offcuts aside for the quilt binding.

UNIT A

**2** Take the other three jelly roll strips and cut a length of 32in from each strip. Sew together lengthways and press the seams in one direction.

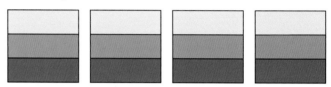

**3** Subcut the strip unit into four 6½in squares – these are unit C – and one 5in square to be set aside for the outer border. Set the offcuts aside for the binding.

UNIT C

5in square

**4** With right sides together, sew a unit A to a unit B. Press the work in the direction shown by the arrow in the diagram below.

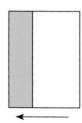

**5** Take a unit C and on the reverse of the fabric draw a diagonal line from corner to corner as shown. Draw another line ½in away from the first line below and to the right of the diagonal as shown.

**6** Pin a unit C right sides together to the AB unit and sew on the drawn lines. Cut between the sewn lines and flip the resulting triangle, pressing towards the triangle. Keep the bonus half-square triangle unit to be used in the outer border.

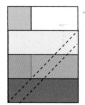

**7** With right sides together, sew a unit D to the right-hand side of the unit as shown. Press the work. This is now a quarter of the block.

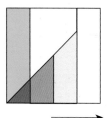

**8** Repeat to make the other three quarters of the block. With right sides together, sew two together as shown and then press.

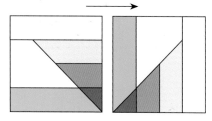

**9** Repeat with the other quarter blocks. Rotate these 180 degrees and sew to the first pair. Press the work.

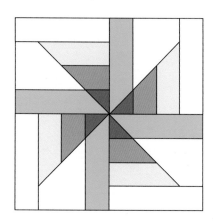

**10** Repeat with seven other piles of strips to complete eight blocks. When cutting for the final ninth block cut the three jelly roll strips 37in long. Sew together lengthwise and cut four C units as before but cut two 5in squares instead of one. You will now have ten 5in squares in total and these will be used for the outer border.

## Assembling the Quilt

Lay out the nine blocks in a pleasing way with three rows of three blocks. Sew the blocks into rows and then sew the three rows together, pinning at all seam intersections to ensure a perfect match. Press the work.

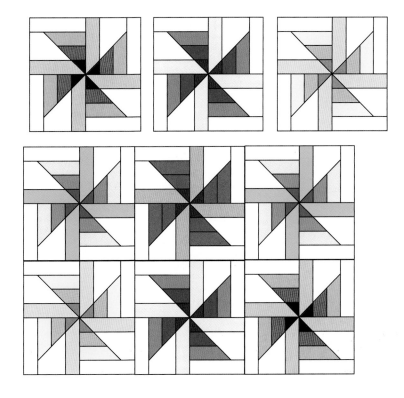

## Sewing the Borders

*Inner border:*

- Take the four lightest jelly roll strips and the background 2½in wide strip set aside for the inner border and subcut each of them into four rectangles 2½in x 10½in. Sew them together to form a continuous length, arranging the pieces by taking one strip from each fabric in turn.
- Determine the vertical measurement from top to bottom through the centre of your quilt top. Cut two side borders to this measurement. Sew to the quilt.
- Now determine the horizontal measurement from side to side across the centre of the quilt top. Cut these two borders to this measurement. Sew to the quilt.

### Outer border:

- Gather all the bonus units from before and press flat. Trim them into 4½in squares, as shown in the diagram below.

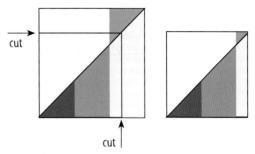

cut

cut

- Take the ten 5in background squares that have been set aside for the outer border and draw from corner to corner on the wrong side.

- With right sides together, pin them to the 5in squares made from the jelly roll strips. Sew a ¼in seam allowance either side of the drawn diagonal line. Cut on the drawn line. Press open and trim to 4½in squares.

- Sew all these units together into two thirteen-unit border strips and two fifteen-unit border strips, positioning corner squares as in the diagram.

## Finishing the Quilt

Your quilt top is now complete. Prepare the top for quilting and then quilt as desired. Bind the quilt to finish (see page 120). Gather all the offcuts and sew into a continuous strip to bind – you will need approximately 250in.

# Birthday Gift Variation>>

We do love a pattern that uses up every last scrap of fabric and to have sufficient fabric for our binding was a real bonus. We especially loved the offcut triangles being trimmed down to make such a great border – be careful to cut them the right way! For our variation we chose a Fig Tree range called Patisserie, which gave a gentle look to the quilt. We are sure that this pattern will be very popular as it is quick and simple to make and makes great use of the jelly roll. Quilt made by Pam and Nicky Lintott and longarm quilted by The Quilt Room.

# Knickerbocker Glory

## Designed by Karen Al-Ghabban

### VITAL STATISTICS

| | |
|---|---|
| Quilt size: | 62in x 54in |
| Block size: | 4in square |
| Number of blocks: | 152 |

"When I saw Heather Bailey's vibrant fabrics, I knew I had to have them! They spoke to me of long, lazy summer days in beautiful gardens exploding with gorgeous blooms. As a relatively new quilter, lacking confidence in my abilities, I found that simplicity was key to a successful design. So I decided not to jumble up the fabrics too much, so that each fabric would have maximum impact. I sketched and abandoned various ideas and finally decided on a four-patch block. After pairing the strips and making the blocks, I laid them out in various formations and particularly liked this 'on point' arrangement." Karen Al-Ghabban

Pam and Nicky's variation quilt shown on page 71 emphasizes the strippy effect of this quilt design, with fabrics chosen to allow the four-patch blocks to stand out.

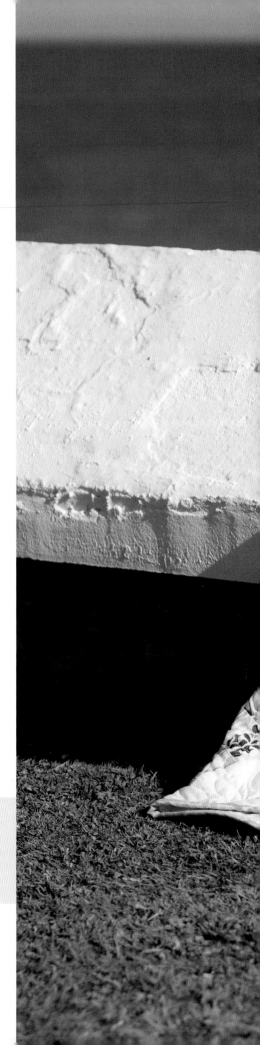

### REQUIREMENTS

- One jelly roll **OR** forty 2½in strips cut across the width of the fabric
- 1yd (1m) of fabric for background squares and setting triangles
- 20in (50cm) of fabric for binding

## Sorting the Jelly Roll Strips

- Sort the jelly roll strips into pairs. You need nineteen pairs – two jelly roll strips are spare. To create the strippy effect try to ensure your pairs are of the same colour, so will contrast with the next strip.
- Read all of the instructions through before starting your quilt. Use a scant ¼in seam allowance throughout.

## Cutting Instructions

### Background fabric:

- Cut five strips 4½in wide across the width of the fabric. Subcut each strip into nine 4½in squares. Set aside thirty-seven for your background squares.
- Take one 4½in square and trim to measure 4in square. Cut across the diagonal to form the two left-hand corner triangles, as shown in the diagram below. (The right-hand corners are formed from setting triangles.) The remaining 4½in squares are spare.

4in square

- Cut two strips 7in wide and subcut each strip into five 7in squares. Cut across both diagonals of each square to form forty setting triangles. Cutting the setting triangles and corner triangles this way ensures the outer edges of your quilt are not on the bias.

7in square

### Binding:

Cut your fabric into seven 2½in wide strips across the width of the fabric.

## Sewing the Four-Patch Blocks

**1** Take one pair of jelly roll strips and with right sides together sew down the long side. Open and press to the darker side.

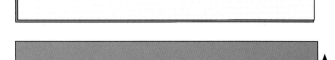

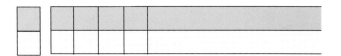

**2** Trim the selvedge and then cut sixteen 2½in wide segments from the strip unit.

**3** Rotate eight of the segments and chain piece together to form eight four-patch blocks, pinning the centre seam to ensure a perfect match.

Four-patch block

**4** Repeat with your other pairs of jelly roll strips, keeping the eight four-patch blocks from each pair of strips in separate piles.

## TIP

When making the four-patch blocks, if you cut each of your jelly roll strip units in half to form two rectangles 4½in x 22in you can layer one half on top of the other, reversing the light and the dark fabric, and cut eight 2½in segments. They are then ready to sew together to form your eight four-patch blocks.

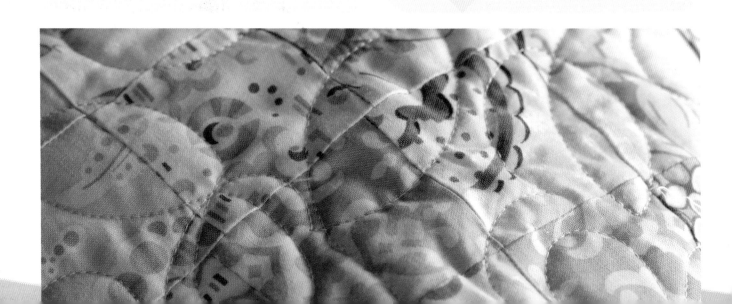

## Assembling the Quilt

- Lay out all the four-patch blocks, background squares and setting triangles as shown in the diagram below, taking great care with the colour placement of your blocks. Starting with row 1, sew a setting triangle to either side of a background square. Continue sewing each row together checking all the time that you have sewn the blocks together correctly. Press the seams of alternate rows in opposite directions to ensure the seams nest together when the rows are sewn together.

- When all the rows are completed, sew them together, pinning at every seam intersection to ensure a perfect match.

## Finishing the Quilt

Your quilt top is now complete. Prepare the top for quilting and quilt as desired. Bind the quilt to finish (see page 120).

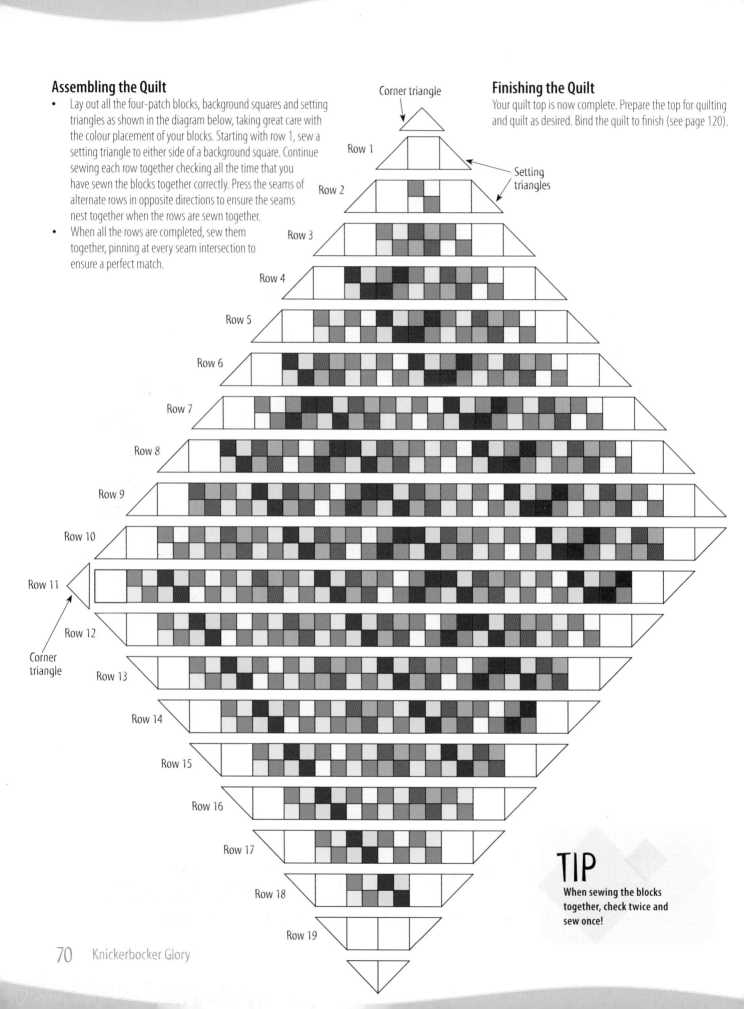

Corner triangle

Row 1

Setting triangles

Row 2

Row 3

Row 4

Row 5

Row 6

Row 7

Row 8

Row 9

Row 10

Row 11

Corner triangle

Row 12

Row 13

Row 14

Row 15

Row 16

Row 17

Row 18

Row 19

## TIP

When sewing the blocks together, check twice and sew once!

# Knickerbocker Glory Variation

A simple four-patch block cleverly set on point creates a strippy effect. The fact that you can make eight four-patch blocks from two jelly roll strips is the essence of this quilt and we really loved it. We thought what a lovely 'first bed' quilt it would make so we chose the bright colours of Mary Engelbrett's range called Baskets of Flowers. We purposely made the strippy effect more distinctive so when choosing our pairs of jelly roll strips to make the four-patch block we chose similar colours, which meant that our four-patch rows stood out more. Quilt made by Pam and Nicky Lintott and longarm quilted by The Quilt Room.

# Candy Heart

## Designed by Pamela Boatright

### VITAL STATISTICS

Quilt size:          54in x 54in
Block size:          11in square
Number of blocks:    12
Setting:             4 x 3 blocks plus borders

"I felt in love with patchwork and quilting over twenty years ago and love designing and making quilts. I work in my local quilt shop in Coos Bay, Oregon and designed this quilt as a shop sample to help sell a new line of jelly rolls. When first asked to create it, I chose this package because I loved the colours in this jelly roll and the coordinating fabric that was available. After unrolling the strips I knew I wanted to make a heart, and since I had already been toying with the idea of making large triangles the design came quickly. Upon seeing my completed quilt, a friend recommended that I enter the Jelly Roll Challenge competition, so I tweaked my design and two tops later came up with my final pattern." Pamela Boatright

For their variation quilt on page 79, Pam and Nicky used a subtle mix of pinks, browns and greys, with the heart in darker shades to emphasize it.

### REQUIREMENTS

- One jelly roll **OR** forty 2½in strips cut across the width of the fabric
- 24in (60cm) of fabric for upper and lower border strips
- 10in (25cm) of fabric for inner border
- 20in (50cm) of fabric for binding

## Sorting the Jelly Roll Strips

- Choose twelve strips for the heart.
- Choose twelve light strips for the background.
- Choose sixteen strips to be used in the chequerboard border, divided into two groups of eight, either by colour or light and dark.
- Read all of the instructions through before starting your quilt. Use a scant ¼in seam allowance throughout.

## Cutting Instructions

### Borders:

- Cut the fabric for upper and lower border strips into three strips 6in wide across the width of the fabric.
- Cut the inner border into five strips 1½in wide across the width of the fabric.

### Binding:

- Cut six strips 2½in wide across the width of the fabric.

## Sewing the Heart Triangle Pieces

**1** Sort the strips allocated for the hearts into three sets of four strips. Sew each set of four strips together, as shown in the diagram below, to create a strip unit 8½in wide. Check that your measurement is correct and if not you must adjust your seam allowance (see page 114 for seam allowance test). Press seams to one side.

**2** Lay a 12in quilting square on a strip unit and cut four triangles. Handle the triangles carefully as the edges are bias and will stretch out of shape easily – a little spray starch when pressing will help keep them from stretching. Repeat with the other two strip units. You need twelve heart triangles.

## TIP

If you only have a 12½in quilting square, use a line of tape to mark the 12in line.

**3** Repeat with the twelve background jelly roll strips to create twelve background triangles.

**4** Sew eight heart triangles to eight background triangles. Carefully press the centre seam to the heart side of the square. Trim the squares to 11½in.

**5** Sew two sets of heart triangles together and two sets of background triangles together. Press centre seams and trim squares to 11½in.

## Assembling the Quilt

- Referring to the diagram below, sew twelve blocks to form the heart, placing the two sets of heart squares at the centre of the heart and the background squares at the bottom corners of the heart. Pin at every intersection to ensure a perfect match. Press gently.

## TIP

Be very careful as you sew the quilt blocks together not to stretch the bias edges of the blocks or handle them more than necessary.

## Adding the Upper and Lower Strips

**1** Cut one 6in border strip in half to create two lengths 6in x 22in and sew one half to each of the remaining 6in border strips. Cut each to measure 44½in and sew on to the top and bottom of your strip heart to make a 44½in square, pinning and easing where necessary. Press towards the borders.

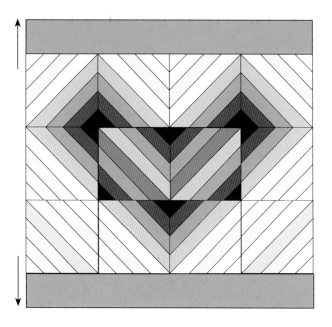

**2** Take one 1½in inner border strip and cut it into four 10in sections. Sew one 10in section to each of the remaining four 1½in border strips. From these border strips, cut two 44½in lengths and sew to the sides of the heart. Now cut two 46½in lengths and sew to the top and bottom of the heart, pinning and easing where necessary.

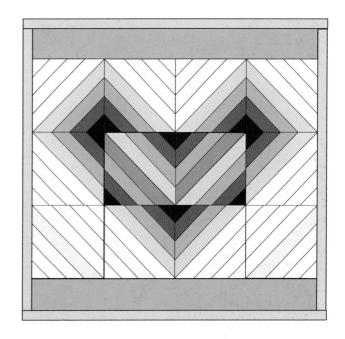

## Adding the Chequerboard Border

**1** Take eight of the jelly roll strips allocated for the chequerboard border and sew into a strip unit of eight, alternating colours or light and dark. Press in one direction. Cut in half so you have two sets of eight strips 22in x 16½in.

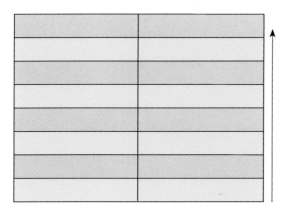

**2** With right sides together, sew these two strips together making sure you continue the colour pattern. Do not press open. Leave right sides together and cut eight 2½in segments across the sewn strips.

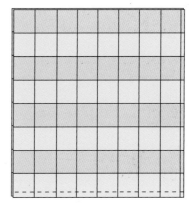

**3** Sew these strips together in pairs, keeping the continuity of the pattern. Remove nine squares from one end of each of two strips and five squares from one end of two strips. Measure these strips – the shorter ones should measure 46½in and the longer strips should measure 54½in. Make any adjustments needed to achieve these measurements.

**4** Repeat with the remaining eight jelly roll strips to create two more 46½in lengths and two more 54½in lengths.

# TIP

**For the chequerboard border, it is especially important to sew an accurate ¼in seam so that the border will match the measurements of your quilt. Sewing a scant ¼in is desired as you can more easily adjust to make the strip smaller than to make it longer. Also, decrease your stitch length to make the seams more stable, as you will be cutting across them.**

**5** Sew one of the 46½in lengths from the first set of chequerboard strips to one from the second set, matching seams and making sure to alternate colours to create the chequerboard pattern.

**6** Pin and sew a chequerboard border to each side of the heart, easing if necessary. Press to the outside. Repeat with the 54½in border lengths and pin and sew to the top and bottom of the heart. Press the work.

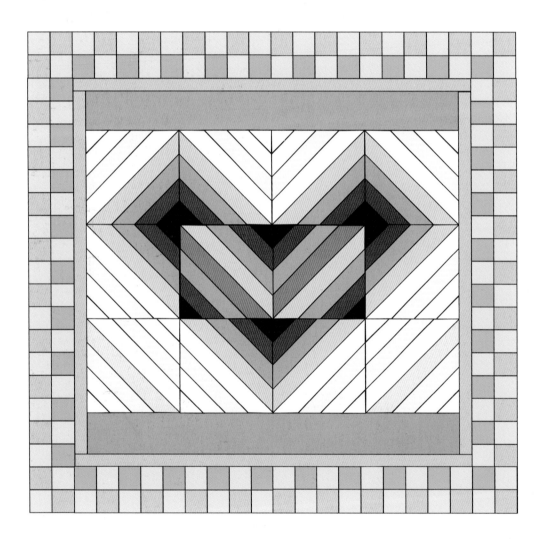

## Finishing the Quilt

Your quilt top is now complete. Prepare the top for quilting and then quilt as desired. Bind the quilt to finish (see page 120).

## Candy Heart Variation

Now this really is a quilt to show how much you love someone. We can imagine many proud mothers and grandmothers around the world making this for a favourite child or grandchild. It would be a lovely quilt for someone to snuggle under and would also make a great play mat. We decided to create a more naïve, primitive-looking quilt and used a Japanese taupe jelly roll with a gorgeous mix of subtle browns, pinks and greys. Quilt made by Pam and Nicky Lintott and longarm quilted by The Quilt Room.

# Zen and the Jelly Roll

## Designed by Laura Paulu

### VITAL STATISTICS

| | |
|---|---|
| Quilt size: | 66in x 78in |
| Block size: | 12½in square |
| Number of blocks: | 20 |
| Setting: | 4 x 5 blocks plus a 2in border and a 6in border |

"My quilt began with a treasure trove of Japanese woven neutrals I chanced upon at my local quilt shop. The delicacy of colour and softness of hand in these fabrics inspired me to create this design to bring out their lovely understated elegance. The fabrics are equally beautiful on both sides, showing subtle variations of value. Each block is slightly different from all the others and I love the moment when the eight triangles become a block – it's like magic!" Laura Paulu

Pam and Nicky's variation quilt on page 87 shows how different this great design looks with an ultra bright and contemporary palette of colours.

### REQUIREMENTS

- One jelly roll **OR** forty 2½in strips cut across the width of the fabric
- 1¼yd (1.25m) of fabric for accent fabric and inner border
- 1½yd (1.5m) of fabric for outer border
- 24in (60cm) of fabric for binding

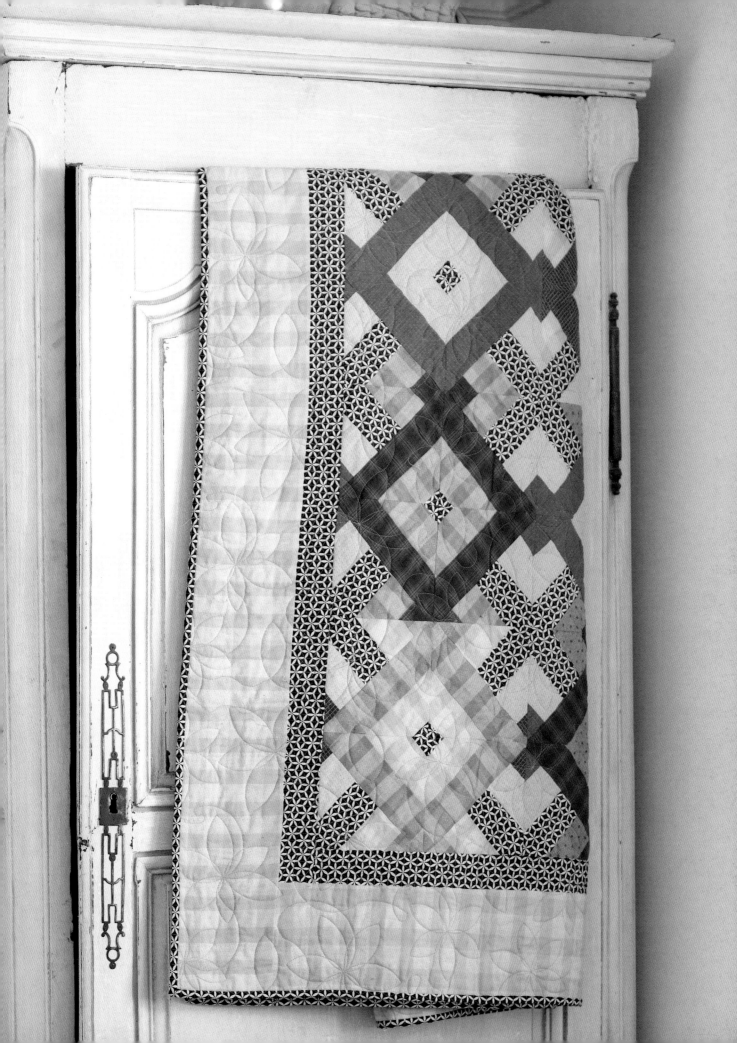

## Sorting the Jelly Roll Strips

- Sort the strips into half light and half dark.
- Read all of the instructions through before starting your quilt. Use a scant ¼in seam allowance throughout.

## Cutting Instructions

### Accent fabric:
- Cut sixteen strips 6½in wide across the width of the fabric. Set six aside for the inner border.

### Outer border:
- Cut eight strips 2½in wide across the width of the fabric.

### Binding:
- Cut into eight 2½in wide strips across the width of the fabric.

## Sewing the Strip Units

**1** Take two light and two dark jelly roll strips and one accent strip and sew them together lengthwise as shown in the diagram below. The order will be dark, light, accent, light and dark. Press seams in one direction.

# TIP

**To stop the strips from bowing, sew them together in alternate directions and press the seam after each strip is added. Repeat until you have ten strip units.**

**2** Take one of the strip units and cut it into four 10½in squares. Ensure you are always cutting at a right angle by keeping the ruler markings along the seam lines and straighten up the cutting edge if necessary. You have very little wastage so cut carefully.

10½in square

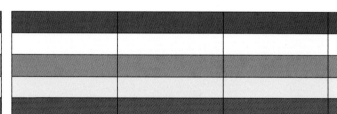

**3** Repeat with each of the strip units. You will have forty 10½in squares in total. Keep the four squares from each strip unit together until you are ready to cut them to construct the blocks.

**4** Take four 10½in squares from one strip unit and cut each square twice on the diagonal. For accuracy it is best to cut them one at a time, rather than stacking them. Label the triangles as shown in the diagram below.

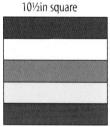

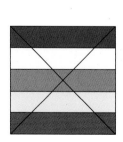

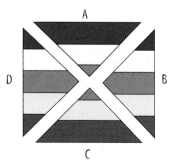

## Sewing the Blocks

**1** From one strip set, take four A triangles and arrange them in a diamond (i.e. on point) on your cutting mat or design wall. Place two B triangles on opposite corners of the diamond and two D triangles on the remaining corners as shown. This will form Block A.

Block A

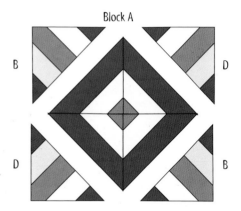

**2** Using the remaining triangles from the same strip set, take four C triangles and arrange them in a diamond, placing two B triangles on opposite corners of the diamond and two D triangles on the remaining corners as shown. This will form Block B.

Block B

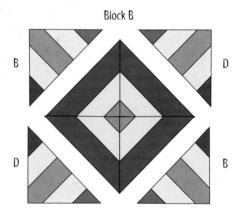

# TIP
**Try to keep your patchwork neat and tidy by snipping threads as you proceed.**

**3** Starting with Block A, sew each corner triangle to the centre on-point triangle adjacent to it to make quarter block units. Gently press the seam so that it is parallel to the other pressed seam.

**4** Sew together the quarter blocks to make half blocks, pinning at every seam intersection to ensure a perfect match. You will find it easier to match and start sewing from the small triangle end. Press the work.

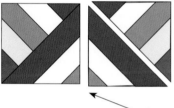

Start sewing from this end

**5** Repeat with the other quarter blocks to form half blocks and then sew the half blocks together, ensuring the seams are pressed in opposite directions so they nest together nicely when sewn. Press blocks gently and, if necessary, square up and trim to 13in square. Block A is now complete.

**6** Repeat the above process to complete Block B, pinning at every seam intersection to ensure a perfect match.

**7** Repeat with the next four 10½in squares from one strip unit, cutting and labelling the triangles and then following steps 1–6 above to assemble blocks A and B. Continue with the remaining 10½in squares until you have in total ten Block As and ten Block Bs.

## Assembling the Quilt

- Referring to the diagram below, sew the blocks together, alternating Blocks A and B to form five rows of four blocks and then sew the rows together, pinning at every seam intersection to ensure a perfect match.

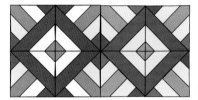

# TIP

**At all times treat the fabric with care as you are dealing with many bias edges. Always press gently and do not use steam.**

## Adding the Borders

- Join the remaining six 2½in strips of accent fabric into a continuous length. Determine the vertical measurement from top to bottom through the centre of your quilt top. Cut two side borders to this measurement. Pin and sew to the quilt, easing if necessary. Press to the border fabric.
- Now determine the horizontal measurement from side to side across the centre of the quilt top. Cut two borders to this measurement. Pin and sew to the quilt. Press to the border fabric.
- Join the eight outer border strips into a continuous length and repeat the process to add the second border.

## Finishing the Quilt

Your quilt top is now complete. Prepare the top for quilting and then quilt as desired. Bind the quilt to finish (see page 120).

## Zen and the Jelly Roll Variation >>

In our book *Layer Cake, Jelly Roll and Charm Quilts* we made a quilt using a complicated pattern from Mary Ellen Hopkins called Hidden Wells, which we loved. This design looks stunning and is less complex so that's got to be a bonus! As Laura's quilt is in sophisticated taupes, we chose to use the 'funky' fabrics from the Oh-Cherry-Oh jelly roll by Me & My Sister and for our accent fabric we used a lilac dot. Sophisticated this is *not* - but it would certainly brighten any bedroom and bring a smile to your face the moment you woke up. We decided to omit the outer border as we liked the quilt just the way it looked. Quilt made by Pam and Nicky Lintott and longarm quilted by The Quilt Room.

# Jelly Roll Bargello

## Designed by Marion Brown

### VITAL STATISTICS
Quilt size: 67in x 55in
Setting: 49 rows plus1in border and 2½in border

"I started quilting twelve years ago and was immediately addicted – my first project was supposed to be just a small lap quilt but ended up king size! Since then I haven't stopped sewing. Bargello quilts have always been one of my favourites and I've made a few in the past, loving the way the patterns undulate. For this quilt I wanted something a little different and more abstract so I chose rich colours with touches of gold. The pattern looks complicated but is easy to follow if you use the piecing diagram on page 92. I really enjoyed making the quilt and hope you do too." Marion Brown

Pam and Nicky's variation on page 95 took boldness and brightness one stage further with a zingy collection of Kaffe Fasset fabrics. A point to bear in mind is that Marion's jelly roll had ten different fabrics, with four strips of each fabric while Pam and Nicky's jelly roll had forty different fabrics. They couldn't make as many rows as Marion did and their quilt ended up slightly smaller but still looked beautiful.

### REQUIREMENTS
- One jelly roll **OR** forty 2½in strips cut across the width of the fabric
- 12in (30cm) each of three coordinating fabrics
- 12in (30cm) of fabric for inner border
- 20in (50cm) of fabric for outer border
- 20in (50cm) of fabric for binding

## Sorting the Jelly Roll Strips

- Sort your jelly roll into ten piles of four fabrics, each pile containing fabrics of the same colour. Be guided by your jelly roll and if some piles are the same colour that doesn't matter – just make sure you don't place them next to each other.
- Read all of the instructions through before starting your quilt. Use a scant ¼in seam allowance throughout.

## Cutting Instructions

### Coordinating fabrics:
- From each of the 12in coordinating fabrics cut four 2½in strips across the width of the fabric to create three further piles of strips.

### Border fabric:
- From the inner border fabric, cut six strips 1½in wide across the width of the fabric.
- From the outer border fabric, cut six strips 3in wide across the width of the fabric.

### Binding fabric:
- Cut seven 2½in wide strips across the width of the fabric.

# TIP

**When choosing the three extra coordinating fabrics for the variation quilt we chose plains in different colours, which really helped to keep track of where we were when following the bargello pattern.**

## Sewing the Strip Units

**1** Arrange your ten piles of jelly roll strips and three piles of additional strips into order, starting with the darkest colour 1 and going to the lightest colour 13.

**2** Take one strip of fabric from each pile. Starting with the darkest colour, stitch strips 1–7 together (see diagram below), alternating the direction of stitching to avoid warping. Press each colour towards the lightest one.

Unit A (darks)

**3** Repeat the above for colours 8–13. Label both these strip units A. Note: if you were to join all thirteen strips together, you would find that it is too wide for sub-cutting later.

Unit A (lights)

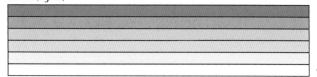

**4** Now make another identical set in the same way. This set also needs to be labelled unit A.

**5** Repeat the above, making two further sets of strip units but, *very importantly*, these must be pressed towards the darkest fabric. Label these Unit B.

Unit B (darks)

Unit B (lights)

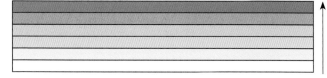

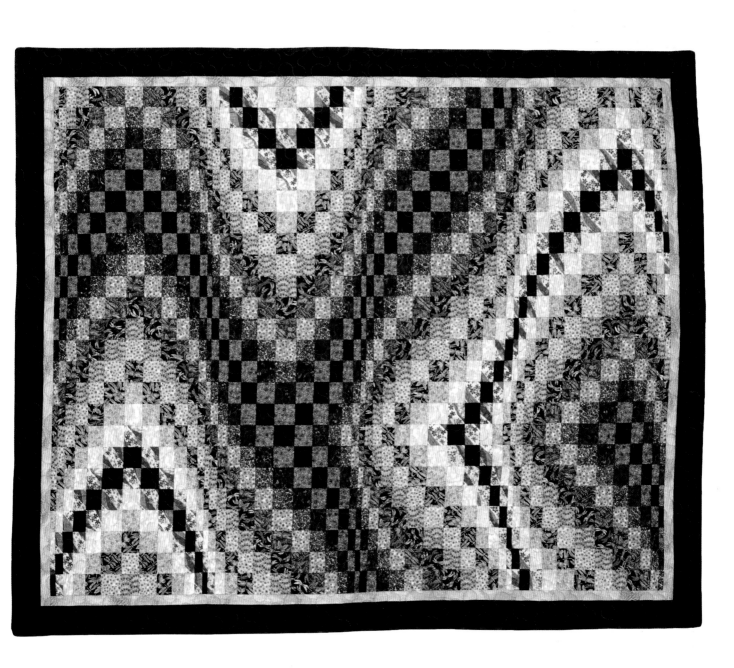

## Cutting the Segments

**1** The strips now are ready to be cut at right angles into rows. Use the piecing chart below to see what width you need to cut each row. The rows are numbered at the top with their width and whether to use Unit A or Unit B is indicated at the bottom of the chart. To make rows 1 to 19 you will need to cut two segments from each unit to complete each row. To make rows 20 onwards, you sometimes need three or four of some of the fabrics.

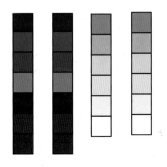

**2** Starting with row 1 and from the A set of strips, cut two segments 1in wide. Following the numbers as shown in the chart, join two segments together to form row 1 (see chart), unpicking the numbers not needed. Keep all your unpicked fabrics as you will need some of them to complete some of the rows later. Your rows will measure approximately 49in.

**3** To make row 2 cut two segments 1¼in wide from the B set of strips.

**4** With right sides together, stitch your first two rows together. The seams will be going in opposite directions, which ensures that they will nest together nicely. Press the work.

**5** Continue in this manner until all 49 rows in the chart have been completed.

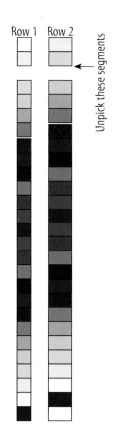

Row 1  Row 2

Unpick these segments

### Piecing chart

| | 1 | 2 | 3 | 4 | 5 | 6 | 7 | 8 | 9 | 10 | 11 | 12 | 13 | 14 | 15 | 16 | 17 | 18 | 19 | 20 | 21 | 22 | 23 | 24 | 25 |
|---|---|---|---|---|---|---|---|---|---|---|---|---|---|---|---|---|---|---|---|---|---|---|---|---|---|
| **Row** | | | | | | | | | | | | | | | | | | | | | | | | | |
| **Width** | 1in | 1¼in | 1½in | 1¾in | 2in | 2¼in | 2½in | 2¼in | 2in | 1¾in | 1½in | 1¼in | 1in | 1¼in | 1½in | 1¾in | 2in | 2¼in | 2½in | 2¼in | 2in | 1¾in | 1½in | 1¼in | 1in |
| **Colour** | 11 | 10 | 9 | 8 | 7 | 6 | 5 | 6 | 7 | 8 | 9 | 10 | 11 | 12 | 13 | 1 | 13 | 12 | 11 | 12 | 13 | 1 | 13 | 12 | 11 |
| | 10 | 9 | 8 | 7 | 6 | 5 | 4 | 5 | 6 | 7 | 8 | 9 | 10 | 11 | 12 | 13 | 1 | 13 | 12 | 13 | 1 | 13 | 12 | 11 | 10 |
| | 9 | 8 | 7 | 6 | 5 | 4 | 3 | 4 | 5 | 6 | 7 | 8 | 9 | 10 | 11 | 12 | 13 | 1 | 13 | 1 | 13 | 12 | 11 | 10 | 9 |
| | 8 | 7 | 6 | 5 | 4 | 3 | 2 | 3 | 4 | 5 | 6 | 7 | 8 | 9 | 10 | 11 | 12 | 13 | 1 | 13 | 12 | 11 | 10 | 9 | 8 |
| | 7 | 6 | 5 | 4 | 3 | 2 | 1 | 2 | 3 | 4 | 5 | 6 | 7 | 8 | 9 | 10 | 11 | 12 | 13 | 12 | 11 | 10 | 9 | 8 | 7 |
| | 6 | 5 | 4 | 3 | 2 | 1 | 2 | 1 | 2 | 3 | 4 | 5 | 6 | 7 | 8 | 9 | 10 | 11 | 12 | 11 | 10 | 9 | 8 | 7 | 6 |
| | 5 | 4 | 3 | 2 | 1 | 2 | 3 | 2 | 1 | 2 | 3 | 4 | 5 | 6 | 7 | 8 | 9 | 10 | 11 | 10 | 9 | 8 | 7 | 6 | 5 |
| | 4 | 3 | 2 | 1 | 2 | 3 | 4 | 3 | 2 | 1 | 2 | 3 | 4 | 5 | 6 | 7 | 8 | 9 | 10 | 9 | 8 | 7 | 6 | 5 | 4 |
| | 3 | 2 | 1 | 2 | 3 | 4 | 5 | 4 | 3 | 2 | 1 | 2 | 3 | 4 | 5 | 6 | 7 | 8 | 9 | 8 | 7 | 6 | 5 | 4 | 3 |
| | 2 | 1 | 2 | 3 | 4 | 5 | 6 | 5 | 4 | 3 | 2 | 1 | 2 | 3 | 4 | 5 | 6 | 7 | 8 | 7 | 6 | 5 | 4 | 3 | 2 |
| | 1 | 2 | 3 | 4 | 5 | 6 | 7 | 6 | 5 | 4 | 3 | 2 | 1 | 2 | 3 | 4 | 5 | 6 | 7 | 6 | 5 | 4 | 3 | 2 | 1 |
| | 2 | 3 | 4 | 5 | 6 | 7 | 8 | 7 | 6 | 5 | 4 | 3 | 2 | 1 | 2 | 3 | 4 | 5 | 6 | 5 | 4 | 3 | 2 | 1 | 2 |
| | 3 | 4 | 5 | 6 | 7 | 8 | 9 | 8 | 7 | 6 | 5 | 4 | 3 | 2 | 1 | 2 | 3 | 4 | 5 | 4 | 3 | 2 | 1 | 2 | 3 |
| | 4 | 5 | 6 | 7 | 8 | 9 | 10 | 9 | 8 | 7 | 6 | 5 | 4 | 3 | 2 | 1 | 2 | 3 | 4 | 3 | 2 | 1 | 2 | 3 | 4 |
| | 5 | 6 | 7 | 8 | 9 | 10 | 11 | 10 | 9 | 8 | 7 | 6 | 5 | 4 | 3 | 2 | 1 | 2 | 3 | 2 | 1 | 2 | 3 | 4 | 5 |
| | 6 | 7 | 8 | 9 | 10 | 11 | 12 | 11 | 10 | 9 | 8 | 7 | 6 | 5 | 4 | 3 | 2 | 1 | 2 | 1 | 2 | 3 | 4 | 5 | 6 |
| | 7 | 8 | 9 | 10 | 11 | 12 | 13 | 12 | 11 | 10 | 9 | 8 | 7 | 6 | 5 | 4 | 3 | 2 | 1 | 2 | 3 | 4 | 5 | 6 | 7 |
| | 8 | 9 | 10 | 11 | 12 | 13 | 1 | 13 | 12 | 11 | 10 | 9 | 8 | 7 | 6 | 5 | 4 | 3 | 2 | 3 | 4 | 5 | 6 | 7 | 8 |
| | 9 | 10 | 11 | 12 | 13 | 1 | 13 | 1 | 13 | 12 | 11 | 10 | 9 | 8 | 7 | 6 | 5 | 4 | 3 | 4 | 5 | 6 | 7 | 8 | 9 |
| | 10 | 11 | 12 | 13 | 1 | 13 | 12 | 13 | 1 | 13 | 12 | 11 | 10 | 9 | 8 | 7 | 6 | 5 | 4 | 5 | 6 | 7 | 8 | 9 | 10 |
| | 11 | 12 | 13 | 1 | 13 | 12 | 11 | 12 | 13 | 1 | 13 | 12 | 11 | 10 | 9 | 8 | 7 | 6 | 5 | 6 | 7 | 8 | 9 | 10 | 11 |
| | 12 | 13 | 1 | 13 | 12 | 11 | 10 | 11 | 12 | 13 | 1 | 13 | 12 | 11 | 10 | 9 | 8 | 7 | 6 | 7 | 8 | 9 | 10 | 11 | 12 |
| | 13 | 1 | 13 | 12 | 11 | 10 | 9 | 10 | 11 | 12 | 13 | 1 | 13 | 12 | 11 | 10 | 9 | 8 | 7 | 8 | 9 | 10 | 11 | 12 | 13 |
| | 1 | 13 | 12 | 11 | 10 | 9 | 8 | 9 | 10 | 11 | 12 | 13 | 1 | 13 | 12 | 11 | 10 | 9 | 8 | 9 | 10 | 11 | 12 | 13 | 1 |
| **Unit** | A | B | A | B | A | B | A | B | A | B | A | B | A | B | A | B | A | B | A | B | A | B | A | B | A |

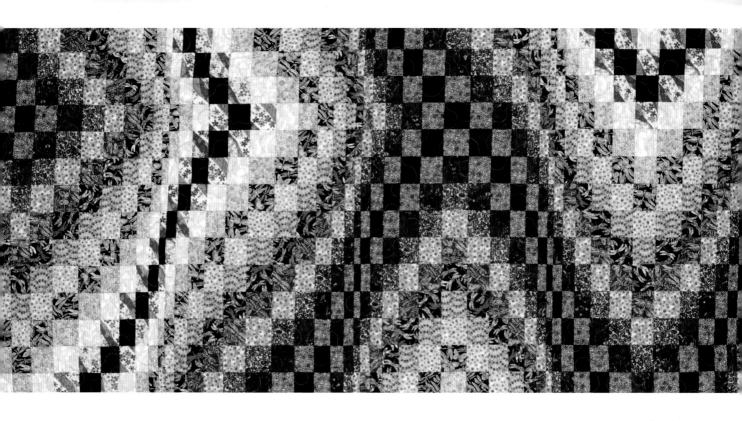

| 26 | 27 | 28 | 29 | 30 | 31 | 32 | 33 | 34 | 35 | 36 | 37 | 38 | 39 | 40 | 41 | 42 | 43 | 44 | 45 | 46 | 47 | 48 | 49 |
|---|---|---|---|---|---|---|---|---|---|---|---|---|---|---|---|---|---|---|---|---|---|---|---|
| 1¼in | 1½in | 1¾in | 2in | 2¼in | 2½in | 2¼in | 2in | 1¾in | 1½in | 1¼in | 1in | 1¼in | 1½in | 1¾in | 2in | 2¼in | 2½in | 2¼in | 2in | 1¾in | 1½in | 1¼in | 1in |
| 10 | 9 | 8 | 7 | 6 | 5 | 4 | 3 | 2 | 1 | 2 | 3 | 4 | 5 | 6 | 7 | 8 | 9 | 10 | 11 | 10 | 9 | 8 | 7 |
| 9 | 8 | 7 | 6 | 5 | 4 | 3 | 2 | 1 | 2 | 3 | 4 | 5 | 6 | 7 | 8 | 9 | 10 | 11 | 12 | 11 | 10 | 9 | 8 |
| 8 | 7 | 6 | 5 | 4 | 3 | 2 | 1 | 2 | 3 | 4 | 5 | 6 | 7 | 8 | 9 | 10 | 11 | 12 | 13 | 12 | 11 | 10 | 9 |
| 7 | 6 | 5 | 4 | 3 | 2 | 1 | 2 | 3 | 4 | 5 | 6 | 7 | 8 | 9 | 10 | 11 | 12 | 13 | 1 | 13 | 12 | 11 | 10 |
| 6 | 5 | 4 | 3 | 2 | 1 | 2 | 3 | 4 | 5 | 6 | 7 | 8 | 9 | 10 | 11 | 12 | 13 | 1 | 13 | 1 | 13 | 12 | 11 |
| 5 | 4 | 3 | 2 | 1 | 2 | 3 | 4 | 5 | 6 | 7 | 8 | 9 | 10 | 11 | 12 | 13 | 1 | 13 | 12 | 13 | 1 | 13 | 12 |
| 4 | 3 | 2 | 1 | 2 | 3 | 4 | 5 | 6 | 7 | 8 | 9 | 10 | 11 | 12 | 13 | 1 | 13 | 12 | 11 | 12 | 13 | 1 | 13 |
| 3 | 2 | 1 | 2 | 3 | 4 | 5 | 6 | 7 | 8 | 9 | 10 | 11 | 12 | 13 | 1 | 13 | 12 | 11 | 10 | 11 | 12 | 13 | 1 |
| 2 | 1 | 2 | 3 | 4 | 5 | 6 | 7 | 8 | 9 | 10 | 11 | 12 | 13 | 1 | 13 | 12 | 11 | 10 | 9 | 10 | 11 | 12 | 13 |
| 1 | 2 | 3 | 4 | 5 | 6 | 7 | 8 | 9 | 10 | 11 | 12 | 13 | 1 | 13 | 12 | 11 | 10 | 9 | 8 | 9 | 10 | 11 | 12 |
| 2 | 3 | 4 | 5 | 6 | 7 | 8 | 9 | 10 | 11 | 12 | 13 | 1 | 13 | 12 | 11 | 10 | 9 | 8 | 7 | 8 | 9 | 10 | 11 |
| 3 | 4 | 5 | 6 | 7 | 8 | 9 | 10 | 11 | 12 | 13 | 1 | 13 | 12 | 11 | 10 | 9 | 8 | 7 | 6 | 7 | 8 | 9 | 10 |
| 4 | 5 | 6 | 7 | 8 | 9 | 10 | 11 | 12 | 13 | 1 | 13 | 12 | 11 | 10 | 9 | 8 | 7 | 6 | 5 | 6 | 7 | 8 | 9 |
| 5 | 6 | 7 | 8 | 9 | 10 | 11 | 12 | 13 | 1 | 13 | 12 | 11 | 10 | 9 | 8 | 7 | 6 | 5 | 4 | 5 | 6 | 7 | 8 |
| 6 | 7 | 8 | 9 | 10 | 11 | 12 | 13 | 1 | 13 | 12 | 11 | 10 | 9 | 8 | 7 | 6 | 5 | 4 | 3 | 4 | 5 | 6 | 7 |
| 7 | 8 | 9 | 10 | 11 | 12 | 13 | 1 | 13 | 12 | 11 | 10 | 9 | 8 | 7 | 6 | 5 | 4 | 3 | 2 | 3 | 4 | 5 | 6 |
| 8 | 9 | 10 | 11 | 12 | 13 | 1 | 13 | 12 | 11 | 10 | 9 | 8 | 7 | 6 | 5 | 4 | 3 | 2 | 1 | 2 | 3 | 4 | 5 |
| 7 | 8 | 9 | 10 | 11 | 12 | 13 | 1 | 13 | 12 | 11 | 10 | 9 | 8 | 7 | 6 | 5 | 4 | 3 | 2 | 1 | 2 | 3 | 4 |
| 6 | 7 | 8 | 9 | 10 | 11 | 12 | 13 | 1 | 13 | 12 | 11 | 10 | 9 | 8 | 7 | 6 | 5 | 4 | 3 | 2 | 1 | 2 | 3 |
| 5 | 6 | 7 | 8 | 9 | 10 | 11 | 12 | 13 | 1 | 13 | 12 | 11 | 10 | 9 | 8 | 7 | 6 | 5 | 4 | 3 | 2 | 1 | 2 |
| 4 | 5 | 6 | 7 | 8 | 9 | 10 | 11 | 12 | 13 | 1 | 13 | 12 | 11 | 10 | 9 | 8 | 7 | 6 | 5 | 4 | 3 | 2 | 1 |
| 3 | 4 | 5 | 6 | 7 | 8 | 9 | 10 | 11 | 12 | 13 | 1 | 13 | 12 | 11 | 10 | 9 | 8 | 7 | 6 | 5 | 4 | 3 | 2 |
| 2 | 3 | 4 | 5 | 6 | 7 | 8 | 9 | 10 | 11 | 12 | 13 | 1 | 13 | 12 | 11 | 10 | 9 | 8 | 7 | 6 | 5 | 4 | 3 |
| 1 | 2 | 3 | 4 | 5 | 6 | 7 | 8 | 9 | 10 | 11 | 12 | 13 | 1 | 13 | 12 | 11 | 10 | 9 | 8 | 7 | 6 | 5 | 4 |
| B | A | B | A | B | A | B | A | B | A | B | A | B | A | B | A | B | A | B | A | B | A | B | A |

## Adding the Borders

- Join your six 1½in wide inner border strips into one continuous length. Determine the vertical measurement from top to bottom through the centre of your quilt top. Cut two side borders to this measurement. Sew to the quilt, pinning and easing where necessary.
- Now determine the horizontal measurement from side to side across the centre of the quilt top. Cut these two borders to this measurement. Sew to the quilt.
- Join your six 3in wide outer border strips into one continuous length and add these to the quilt in the same way.

## Finishing the Quilt

Your quilt top is now complete. Prepare the top for quilting and then quilt as desired. Bind the quilt to finish (see page 120).

# TIP

When clearing away after a sewing session it can be difficult to find a suitable storage space for your rotary cutting board. It has to be kept flat and away from direct sunlight, so under the bed is a possibility. Alternatively, you could try hanging it on a skirt hanger and put it safely away in your wardrobe. Okay, it sounds a bit mad but quilters are often a bit mad!

# Jelly Roll Bargello Variation >>

To a non-quilter, bargello patchwork must seem even more strange than regular patchwork! Not only do we cut up fabric to sew together again, we also unpick sewn pieces from one length of patchwork to re-sew on to the other end! Yes – we are all definitely mad. Marion's jelly roll had only ten different fabrics – four strips of each fabric, which gave the quilt a more coordinated look and we needed to make sure that the pattern would work with a regular jelly roll where most of the fabric strips are different. We chose the multicoloured fabrics from Kaffe Fassett and although we found that some of our fabric sets were similar it didn't seem to matter at all. We chose distinctive plain fabrics for our three additional fabrics and this helped immensely when keeping track of the order of fabrics. It is very important to keep all your offcuts as we certainly needed them and occasionally we trimmed some offcuts to the size we wanted. Full marks to Marion for good use of fabric. Quilt made by Pam and Nicky Lintott and longarm quilted by The Quilt Room.

# Be My Valentine

## Designed by Helen Allison

### VITAL STATISTICS
| | |
|---|---|
| Quilt size: | 72in x 72in |
| Block size: | 16in square |
| Number of blocks: | 16 |
| Setting: | 4 x 4 blocks plus two 2in borders (the main pattern extends into the border) |

"I've always liked working with textiles, enjoying their colours, textures and designs, and have found quilt making to be an excellent way of following this interest and being creative. My quilt design came from a combination of things: I'd already bought a Grand Revival jelly roll and the colours suggested a soft, romantic design; quilts were often made as gifts for engagements or weddings and finally, the Jelly Roll competition closing date was Valentine's Day, so I just had to design this Be My Valentine quilt! For accuracy I used templates for cutting out (provided on pages 104–107)." Helen Allison

Pam and Nicky's variation quilt on page 103 also uses the traditional colours of romance, red and cream, but in bolder shades that really make the heart shapes sing. To try out the heart block using a triangular ruler why not make the stylish cushion on page 108 first?

### REQUIREMENTS
- One jelly roll **OR** forty 2½in strips cut across the width of the fabric
- 2¾yd (2.5m) of background fabric
- 24in (60cm) of fabric for binding
- Two sheets of A3 template plastic

## Sorting the Jelly Roll Strips

- Choose sixteen jelly roll strips to make the hearts – it will take one strip to make each heart.
- Choose one strip to make the contrasting squares set into each heart – one strip will make the required sixteen of these.
- The remaining twenty-three strips will be used for the 'flowers' and borders.
- Read all of the instructions through before starting your quilt. Use a scant ¼in seam allowance throughout.
- We have given templates for all the shapes required for the heart block. Templates B, C and G have been coloured in red indicating that, if desired, you do not need to make templates for these shapes as they can be rotary cut.

## Cutting Instructions

### Jelly roll strips:

- Take the one strip chosen for the contrasting square within the heart and cut into sixteen squares 2½in x 2½in.
- Take sixteen of the twenty-three strips allocated for the borders and flowers and cut one rectangle 2½in x 8½in and twelve squares 2½in x 2½in from each. Set the sixteen 2½in x 8½in rectangles aside for the borders. The 192 squares are for the flowers.
- From the remaining seven strips cut each strip into sixteen squares 2½in x 2½in to make a further 112 squares for the flowers. You need a total of 300 squares (you will have four spare). Set these aside for the flowers, keeping the squares from the same fabric together.

### Background fabric:

- Cut thirty-eight strips 2½in wide across the width of the fabric.
- Take two strips and cut each strip into sixteen squares 2½in x 2½in and set aside for the borders.
- Take four strips and cut each strip into one square 2½in x 2½in plus four rectangles 2½in x 8½in and set aside for the borders. You need sixteen rectangles 2½in x 8½in and thirty-six squares 2½in x 2½in.
- The remaining thirty-two strips will be used to make the heart block.

### Binding:

- Cut eight 2½in wide strips across the width of the fabric.

## Making the Heart Blocks

**1** One jelly roll strip and two background strips make a heart block. From the jelly roll strip each heart block requires the following.
Two template A.
One template B (rotary cut).
One template C (rotary cut).
One template D.
One template E.
One template F.

**2** Take one jelly roll strip allocated for the hearts and cut one square 2½in x 2½in (template B) and one rectangle 2½in x 8½in (template C).

**3** On the reverse side of the balance of the strip lay out the templates, reverse side up, as shown in the first diagram below, taking care to place them as near as possible to each other. There is virtually no wastage so make sure you place them as near to each other as possible, rotating them as shown to fit them in. Make sure you *rotate* the templates and not flip them as otherwise you may find you are cutting the reverse shape. When you have checked that you have placed them correctly and that they will all fit on the strip, mark around them and then cut out.

## TIP

To speed up template making, rotary cut the template plastic into 2½in strips, then you only need to trim the ends to size and shape.

**4** From the background strips of fabric each heart block requires the following shapes.
Two template C (rotary cut).
One template G (rotary cut).
One template F.
Two template H.
Two template I.
Two template B (rotary cut).
Two template J.
Two template K.

**5** Take one background strip and rotary cut two rectangles 2½in x 8½in (C), one rectangle 2½in x 12½in (G) and two squares 2½in x 2½in (B), as shown in the second diagram below.

Jelly roll strip

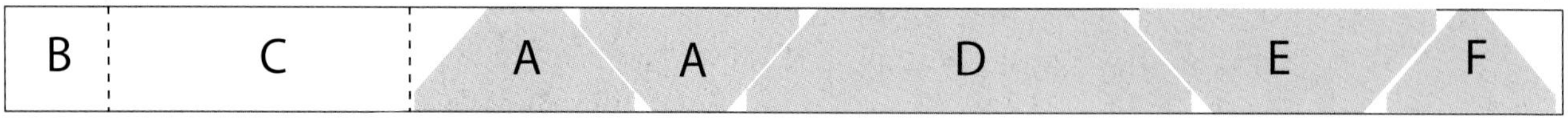

| B | C | A | A | D | E | F |
|---|---|---|---|---|---|---|

Background strip 1

| C | C | G | B | B | spare |
|---|---|---|---|---|---|

**6** Take another background strip and on the reverse lay out the templates, reverse side up, as shown below. Again, make sure you *rotate* the templates and not flip them. When you have checked that you have placed them correctly and that they will all fit on the strip, mark around them and then cut out.

Background strip 2

**7** Referring to the block diagram below, lay out all the pieces as shown to form the heart block. Sew together to form rows, pinning at every seam intersection to ensure a perfect match. Join the rows but at this stage *don't* include the top or bottom two rows as you will need the flowers part of the quilt before you can do that.

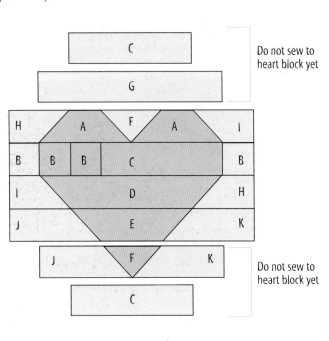

Do not sew to heart block yet

Do not sew to heart block yet

**8** Repeat this process to make sixteen heart blocks, keeping all the partially completed blocks in separate piles.

## TIP

Once you get the hang of it, you can cut out more than one strip at a time by pressing two or three strips together, all with the reverse side upward, and then laying the marked strip on top. Don't cut through more than three or four at a time though as you will lose accuracy.

## Assembling the Quilt

**1** Take the 300 2½in squares allocated for the flowers and borders and sort them into pleasing combinations of four squares from one fabric for the inner part of the flower and eight squares from another fabric for the outer part of the flower. You need twenty-five flower combinations.

**2** Lay out the sixteen (partially completed) heart blocks as shown in the diagram with step 7 opposite. Place some hearts face up, some down, some left and some right.

**3** Arrange the flower squares between the hearts. One quarter of the quilt will look like the diagram below, although it is important to lay out the entire quilt before proceeding with the sewing.

**4** Once you are happy with the layout, complete the heart blocks by finishing the remaining four rows in each one and sewing these rows to the blocks. Each corner of a block will include a quarter of a flower, as shown in the diagram below. Some squares for the edge and corner flowers won't be needed until the final step, which is to add the border – see overleaf.

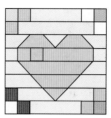

Completed heart block

A quarter of the quilt

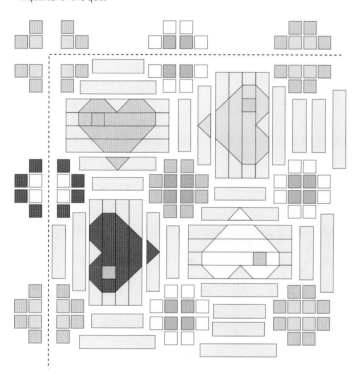

## Adding the Borders

- Using the thirty-six background squares and sixteen background rectangles plus the remaining flower pieces, make up two strips for each side of the quilt and sew them on as shown in the diagram below.
- The 2½in x 8½in rectangles from the jelly roll strips (shown in blue on the diagram) are all in the outer rows, arranged for a pleasing effect.

## Finishing the Quilt

Your quilt top is now complete. Prepare the top for quilting and then quilt as desired. Bind the quilt to finish (see page 120).

# Be My Valentine Variation

Helen used templates for her shapes for accuracy and although we thought we might be able to use the Omnigrid 96 for cutting trapezoid shapes we then realized that her method was the only one that would enable cutting all the shapes from one jelly roll strip for one heart. There is certainly no wastage with this quilt! For our variation we chose a red jelly roll with a cream tone-on-tone background fabric, which we thought was very romantic, and we enhanced it with a heart quilting design. The quilt was made by Pam and Nicky Lintott and longarm quilted by The Quilt Room.

## Templates

The templates for the Be My Valentine quilt are on pages 105–107. All have been produced full size except Template G, which is at 50% and will need to be doubled in size on a photocopier. Templates B, C and G have been tinted red, indicating that, if desired, you do not need to make templates for these shapes as they can be rotary cut. Seam allowances have been included on all templates. See page 116 for advice on using templates.

**This diagram shows an overview of the templates needed for the Be My Valentine quilt - see opposite and overleaf for the actual templates**

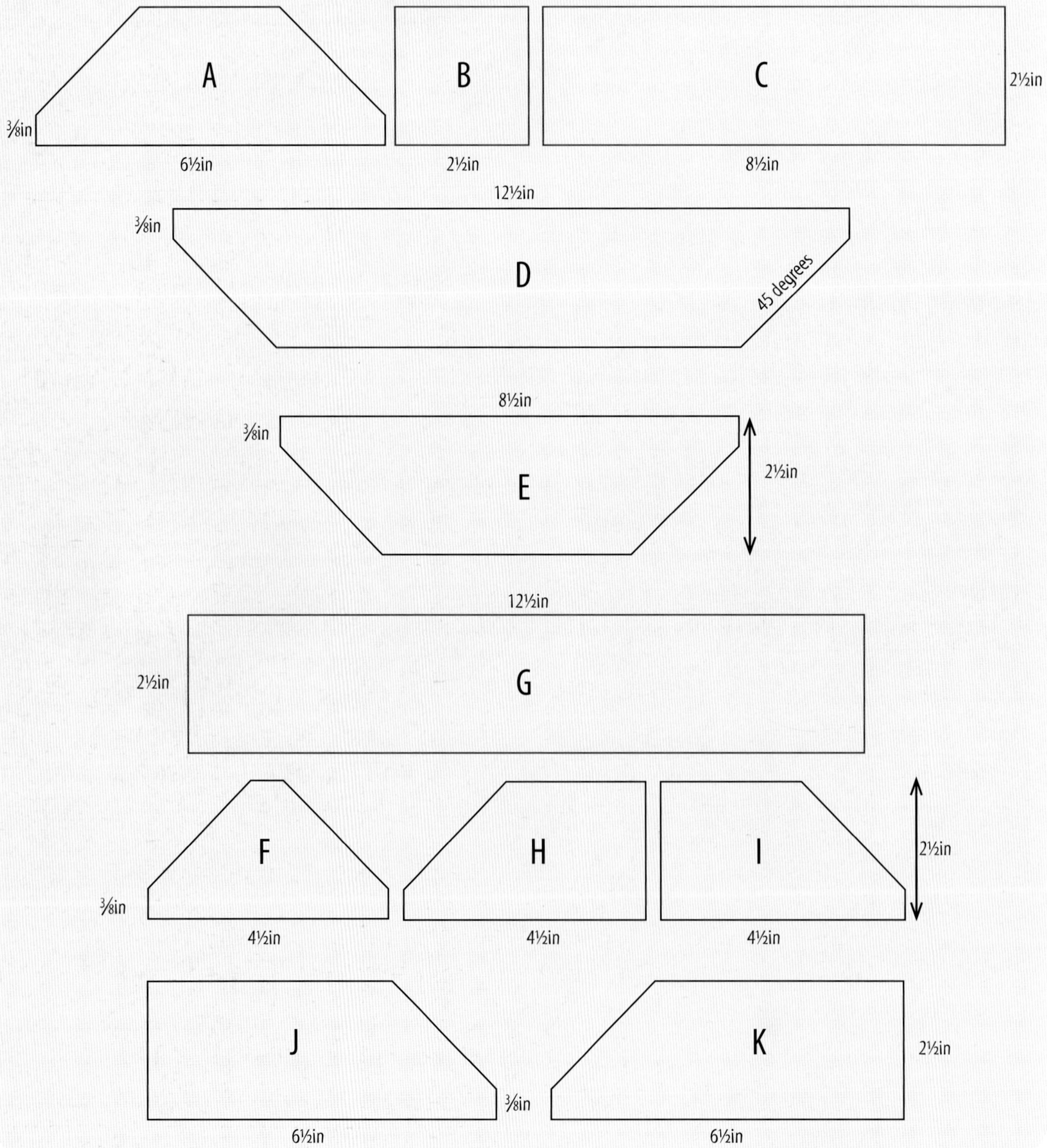

A  ⅜in  6½in

B  2½in

C  8½in  2½in

D  12½in  ⅜in  45 degrees

E  8½in  ⅜in  2½in

G  12½in  2½in

F  4½in  ⅜in

H  4½in

I  4½in  2½in

J  6½in  ⅜in

K  6½in  2½in

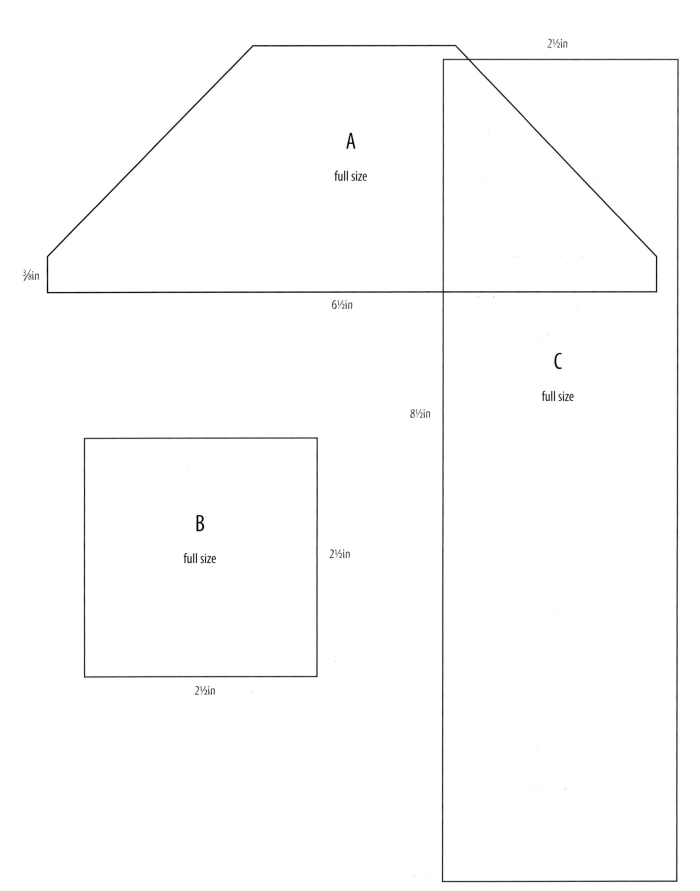

2½in

A

full size

⅜in

6½in

8½in

C

full size

B

full size

2½in

2½in

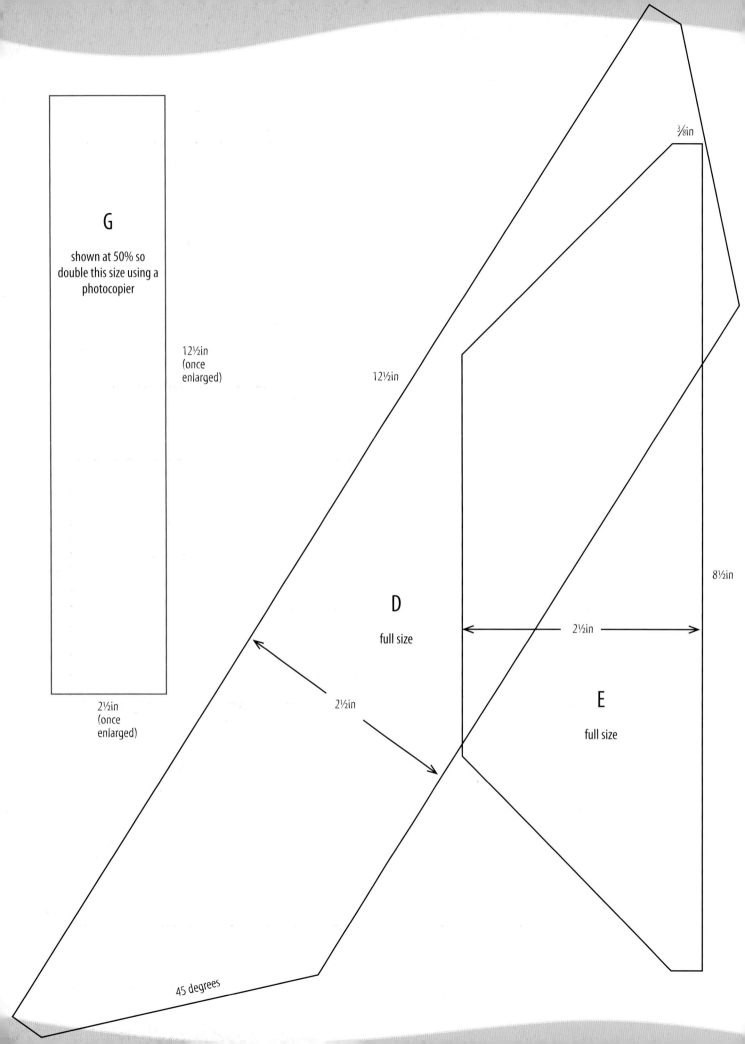

**G**

shown at 50% so double this size using a photocopier

12½in (once enlarged)

2½in (once enlarged)

⅜in

12½in

8½in

**D**

full size

2½in

2½in

**E**

full size

45 degrees

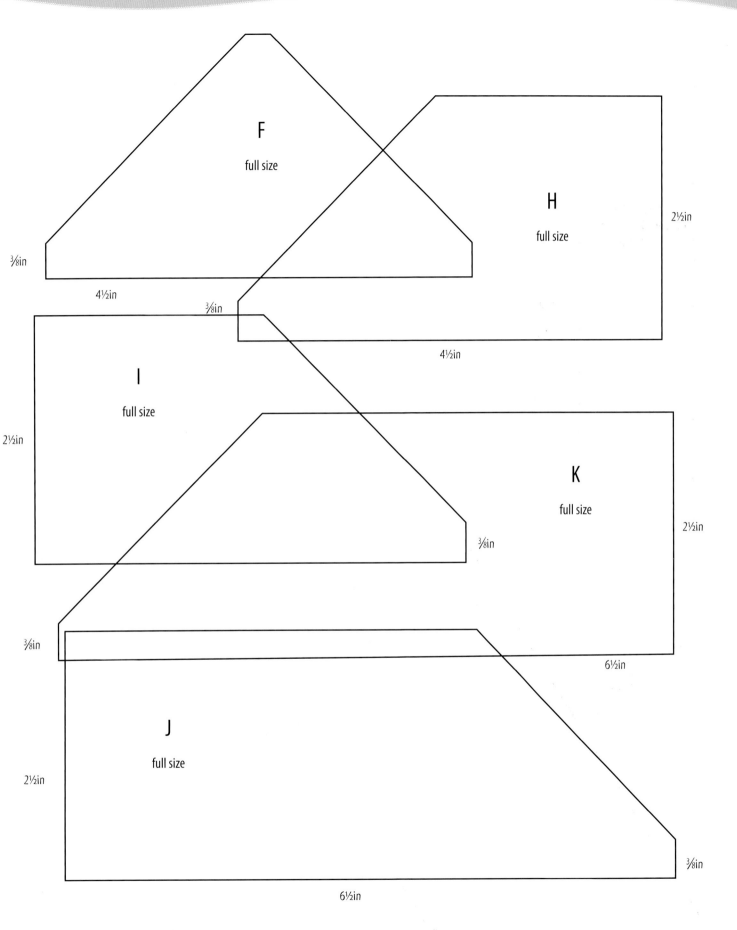

F
full size

H
full size

2½in

⅜in

4½in

⅜in

4½in

I
full size

2½in

K
full size

⅜in

2½in

⅜in

6½in

J
full size

2½in

⅜in

6½in

# Valentine Cushion

## Inspired by the Be My Valentine quilt

### VITAL STATISTICS
Quilt size:        20in x 20in
Block size:       16in square
Number of blocks:  1 heart block plus a 2in border

When we saw all those angles in the Be My Valentine quilt we knew that normally they could be cut with an Omnigrid 96 or similar speciality triangle. However, Helen's gorgeous design to have each heart made from one jelly roll strip meant that rotary cutting with the Omnigrid 96 couldn't be used to cut the shapes as this method does take more fabric. We couldn't resist trying out the design using the Omnigrid 96 which meant using more than one jelly roll strip for each heart. Here is our cushion just to show that it looks equally stunning with different fabrics making up the heart – what a versatile pattern it is. You can either use templates as Helen did or, if you prefer and you have some extra fabric, you could use the Omnigrid 96 to cut the shapes and we have given instructions on how to do that here.

### REQUIREMENTS
- Four jelly roll strips
- Two 2½in background fabric strips cut across the width of the fabric
- Two 2½in strips for border cut across the width of the fabric
- Two pieces of backing fabric 20in x 14in (50cm x 35.5cm)

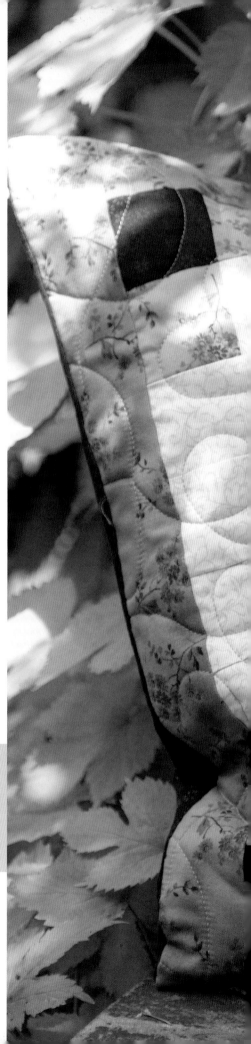

## Sorting the Jelly Roll Strips

- Choose two strips to make the heart.
- Choose one strip to make the contrasting square set into each heart, plus the corner squares.
- Choose one strip to make the dark corner squares.
- Read all of the instructions through before starting your cushion. Use a scant ¼in seam allowance throughout.

## Cutting Instructions

### Jelly roll:

- From one of the strips allocated for the heart cut the following.
  Two rectangles 2½in x 6½in (for template A).
  One rectangle 2½in x 12½in (for template D).
  One rectangle 2½in x 4½in (for template F).
- From the other strip allocated for the heart cut the following.
  One square 2½in x 2½in (for template B).
  Two rectangles 2½in x 8½in (for templates C and E).
- From the strip chosen for the contrasting heart and corners cut nine squares 2½in x 2½in.
- From the dark corner strip cut four squares 2½in x 2½in.

### Background fabric:

- From one background strip cut the following.
  Two rectangles 2½in x 8½in (template C).
  One rectangle 2½in x 12½in (template G).
  Two squares 2½in x 2½in (template B).
  One rectangle 2½in x 4½in (template F).
- From the other background strip cut the following.
  Four rectangles 2½in x 4½in (templates H and I).
  Four rectangles 2½in x 6½in (templates J and K).

### Border fabric:

- Cut each strip into two lengths 2½in x 16in and 2½in x 20in. You may prefer to measure your cushion top when complete before cutting these borders just in case your measurements vary.

## Templates needed for the Valentine Cushion

**A** 6½in, ⅜in
**B** 2½in
**C** 8½in, 2½in
**D** 12½in, ⅜in, 45 degrees
**E** 8½in, ⅜in, 2½in
**G** 2½in, 12½in
**F** 4½in, ⅜in
**H** 4½in
**I** 4½in, 2½in
**J** 6½in, ⅜in
**K** 6½in, 2½in

## Rotary Cutting the Template Shapes

**1** You have all your rectangles cut and you now need to cut the angles to create the correct shapes. Refer to the template diagram shown above, to see what shape is required.

**2** Start with template A and take a 2½in x 6½in rectangle and position the Omnigrid 96 as shown below, with the 6in line at the bottom of the jelly roll strip and aligning the left-hand edge. You use the 6in line because the template is 6½in (finished size 6in). Rotary cut along the ruler to create the right hand 45 degree angle.

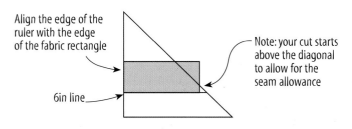

Align the edge of the ruler with the edge of the fabric rectangle

Note: your cut starts above the diagonal to allow for the seam allowance

6in line

**3** Turn the fabric so that the reverse is uppermost and do the same on the other side. You have now cut template A.

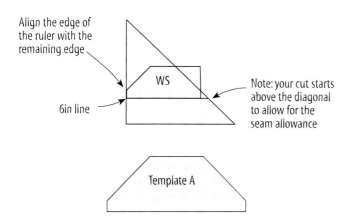

Align the edge of the ruler with the remaining edge

6in line

WS

Note: your cut starts above the diagonal to allow for the seam allowance

Template A

**4** Repeat this process to make all the other templates, positioning the 4in line at the bottom of the strip when cutting the 4½in templates. Leave the larger ones to last as by that time you will know where to position the ruler as you won't have the left-hand side to align. Take care to cut the angles on the correct side of the fabric.

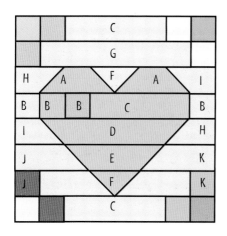

**5** You can now follow the instructions for one block from the quilt instructions (step 7 on page 100), adding the corner squares and then the border. Quilt if desired and then make up as a cushion.

## Making up an Envelope Cushion Cover

**1** Take your two pieces of backing fabric and hem one long end of each backing piece.

**2** With right sides together lay both backing pieces on to the pieced top and pin in place. The backing pieces will overlap at the centre by about 4in. Sew the seams using a generous ¼in seam allowance.

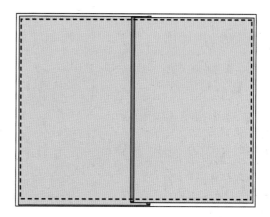

**3** Turn the cushion cover right sides out and press. Insert a cushion pad to finish.

# General Techniques

## Tools

All the projects in this book require rotary cutting equipment. You will need a self-healing cutting mat at least 18in x 24in and a rotary cutter. We recommend the 45mm or the 60mm rotary cutter.

Any rotary cutting work requires rulers and most people have a make they prefer. We like the Creative Grids rulers (see page 127 for contact details) as their markings are clear, they do not slip on the fabric and their Turn-a-Round facility is so useful when dealing with half-inch measurements. We recommend the 6½in x 24in as a basic ruler plus a large square no less than 12½in, which is handy for squaring up and making sure you are always cutting at right angles.

We have tried not to use too many different speciality rulers but when working with 2½in strips you do have to rethink some cutting procedures. The Omnigrid 96 or the larger 96L is widely available from quilting suppliers. It is used for cutting half-square triangles from jelly roll strips as shown in Peace Medallion and also for making the angled shapes in the Be My Valentine cushion. If you are using any other tool, please make sure you are lining up your work on the correct markings.

### Basic tool kit

- Tape measure
- Rotary cutter
- Cutting ruler
- Cutting mat
- Needles
- Pins
- Scissors
- Pencil
- Fabric marker
- Iron
- Sewing machine

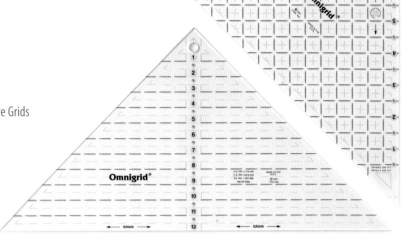

We all have our favourite rulers. We like the use the Creative Grids rulers and squares, some of which are shown here.

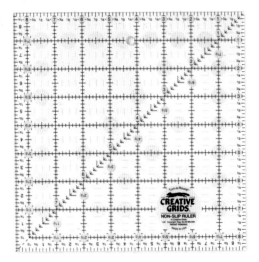

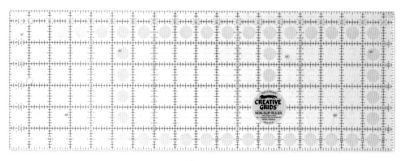

# Seams

We cannot stress enough the importance of maintaining an accurate ¼in seam allowance throughout. We prefer to say an accurate **scant** ¼in seam because there are two factors to take into consideration. Firstly, the thickness of thread and secondly when you press your seam allowance to one side, it takes up a tiny amount of fabric which has to be taken into consideration. These are both extremely small amounts but if they are ignored you will find your *exact* ¼in seam allowance is taking up more than ¼in. So, it is well worth testing your seam allowance before starting on a quilt and most sewing machines have various needle positions that can be used to make any adjustments.

## Seam allowance test

Take a 2½in strip and cut off three segments 1½in wide. Sew two segments together down the longer side and press the seam to one side. Sew the third segment across the top. It should fit exactly. If it doesn't, you need to make an adjustment to your seam allowance. If it is too long, your seam allowance is too wide and can be corrected by moving the needle on your sewing machine to the right. If it is too small, your seam allowance is too narrow and can be corrected by moving the needle to the left.

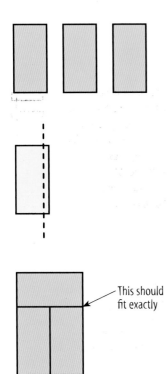

This should fit exactly

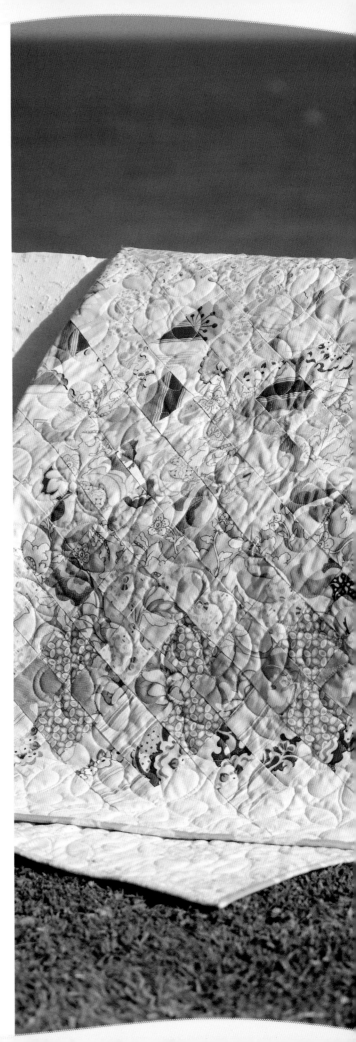

# Pressing

In quiltmaking, pressing is of vital importance and if extra care is taken you will be well rewarded. This is especially true when dealing with strips. If your strips start bowing and stretching you will lose accuracy.

- Always set your seam after sewing by pressing the seam as sewn, without opening up your strips. This eases any tension and prevents the seam line from distorting. Move the iron with an up and down motion, zigzagging along the seam rather than ironing down the length of the seam which could cause distortion.

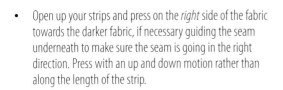

- Open up your strips and press on the *right* side of the fabric towards the darker fabric, if necessary guiding the seam underneath to make sure the seam is going in the right direction. Press with an up and down motion rather than along the length of the strip.

- Always take care if using steam and certainly don't use steam anywhere near a bias edge.
- When you are joining more than two strips together, press the seams after attaching *each* strip. You are far more likely to get bowing if you leave it until your strip unit is complete before pressing.
- Each seam must be pressed flat before another seam is sewn across it. Unless there is a special reason for not doing so, seams are pressed towards the darker fabric. The main criteria when joining seams, however, is to have the seam allowances going in the opposite direction to each other as they then nest together without bulk. Your patchwork will lie flat and your seam intersections will be accurate.

# Pinning

Don't underestimate the benefits of pinning. When you have to align a seam it is important to insert pins to stop any movement when sewing. Long, fine pins with flat heads are recommended as they will go through the layers of fabric easily and allow you to sew up to and over them.

Seams should always be pressed in opposite directions so they will nest together nicely. Insert a pin either at right angles or diagonally through the seam intersection ensuring that the seams are matching perfectly. When sewing, do not remove the pin too early as your fabric might shift and your seams will not be perfectly aligned.

# Chain Piecing

Chain piecing is the technique of feeding a series of pieces through the sewing machine without lifting the presser foot and without cutting the thread between each piece. Always chain piece when you can as it saves time and thread. Once your chain is complete simply snip the thread between the pieces.

When chain piecing shapes other than squares and rectangles it is sometimes preferable when finishing one shape to lift the presser foot slightly and reposition on the next shape, still leaving the thread uncut.

# Removing Dog Ears

A dog ear is the excess piece of fabric which overlaps past the seam allowance when sewing triangles to other shapes. Dog ears should always be cut off to reduce bulk. They can be trimmed using a rotary cutter although snipping with small sharp scissors is quicker. Make sure you are trimming the points parallel to the straight edge of the triangle

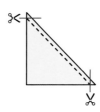

# Using Templates

If you are using templates to make your blocks as in the Be My Valentine quilt, a template will be needed for each different shape used in the blocks. Templates should be made from template plastic and they should include a ¼in seam allowance all round.

Mark each template with the name of the block, its finished size and an identifying letter. Do this on the right side of the template, so that you have an instant check on which way up it should be. This is particularly necessary with asymmetrical shapes. Keep organized and store all the templates for a particular block together labelled with the name and size plus a drawing of the block with each patch lettered.

To cut out your fabric from the templates, lay the pressed fabric out flat, reverse side up. Place the template on the reverse of the fabric and, using a hard lead pencil, draw around the template carefully, taking particular care at points and corners. Do not include a selvedge, either in a patch or its seam allowance. For the most economical use of fabric, cut the patches close together unless you want to 'fussy cut' a particular piece, in which case place the template over that particular piece.

# Fusible Web Appliqué

Appliqué means attaching pieces of fabric to a background fabric and there are various ways to do this. We describe here how do fusible web appliqué, which we have used in our variation of the quilt May Flowers. You would normally have to make sure that the templates you are using have been reversed, because you will be drawing the shape on the back of the fabric. However, as the flower template in May Flowers was the same both ways we didn't have to worry about reversing the template for this quilt.

**1** Reverse the templates (if necessary) and using a light source, such as a light box or a window, trace around each shape on to the paper side of the fusible webbing.

**2** Cut out around each shape and iron the fusible webbing on to the wrong side of the appropriate fabrics, paper side up, and cut out accurately.

**3** When cool, peel the backing paper from the fusible webbing and position the appliqué shape in place, right side up. Press with a hot iron.

**4** You can then choose to sew around the edges of the appliqué to secure in place either by hand or by machine. A satin stitch is often used when sewing by machine and a blanket stitch when edging by hand.

## Joining Border and Binding Strips

If you need to join strips for your borders and binding, you may choose to join them with a diagonal seam to make them less noticeable. When all strips are joined press the seams open.

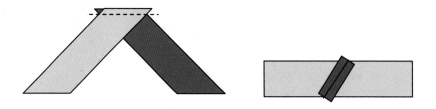

# Adding Borders

The fabric requirements in this book all assume you are going to be sewing straight rather than mitred borders. If you intend to have mitred borders please add sufficient fabric for this (see instructions, right).

## Adding straight borders

**1** Determine the vertical measurement from top to bottom through the centre of your quilt top. Cut two side border strips to this measurement. Mark the halves and quarters of one quilt side and one border with pins. Placing right sides together and matching the pins, stitch the quilt and border together, easing the quilt side to fit where necessary. Repeat on the opposite side. Press open.

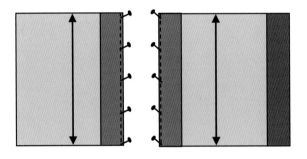

**2** Now determine the horizontal measurement from side to side across the centre of the quilt top. Cut two top and bottom border strips to this measurement and add to the quilt top in the same manner.

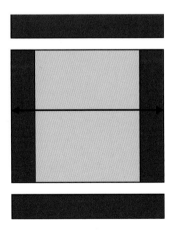

## Adding mitred borders

If you wish to create mitred borders rather than straight borders follow these instructions.

**1** Measure the length and width of the quilt and cut two border strips the length of the quilt *plus* twice the width of the border and cut two border strips the width of the quilt *plus* twice the width of the border.

**2** Sew the border strips to the quilt beginning and ending ¼in away from the corners, backstitching to secure at either end. Begin your sewing right next to where you have finished sewing your previous border but ensure your stitching doesn't overlap. When you have sewn your four borders, press and lay the quilt out on a flat surface, with the reverse side of the quilt uppermost.

**3** Fold the top border up and align it with the side border. Press the resulting 45 degree line that starts at the ¼in stop and runs to the outside edge of the border.

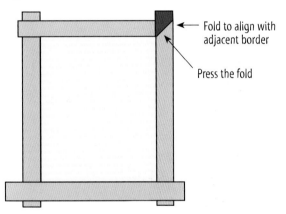

Fold to align with adjacent border

Press the fold

**4** Now lift the side border above the top border and fold it to align with the top border. Press it to create a 45 degree line. Repeat with all four corners.

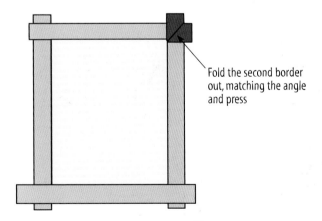

Fold the second border out, matching the angle and press

**5** Align the horizontal and vertical borders in one corner by folding the quilt diagonally and stitch along the pressed 45 degree line to form the mitre, back stitching at either end. Trim the excess border fabric ¼in from your sewn line. Repeat with the other three corners.

# Quilting

Quilting stitches hold the patchwork top, wadding and backing together and create texture over your finished patchwork. The choice is yours whether you hand quilt, machine quilt or send it off to a longarm quilting service. There are many books dedicated to the techniques of hand and machine quilting but the basic procedure is as follows.

**1** With the aid of templates or a ruler, mark out the quilting lines on the patchwork top using your favourite marking technique.

**2** Cut the backing and wadding at least 3in larger all around than the patchwork top. Pin or tack the layers together to prepare them for quilting.

**3** Quilt either by hand or by machine. The aim is to have short, evenly spaced stitches.

# Binding a Quilt

The fabric requirements in this book are for a 2½in double-fold French binding cut on the straight of grain.

**1** Trim the excess backing and wadding (batting) so that the edges are even with the top of the quilt.

**2** Join your binding strips into a continuous length, making sure there is sufficient to go around the quilt plus 8in–10in for the corners and overlapping ends.

**3** With wrong sides together, press the binding in half lengthways. Fold and press under ½in to neaten the edge at the end where you will start sewing.

**4** On the right side of the quilt and starting about 12in away from a corner, align the edges of the double thickness binding with the edge of the quilt so that the cut edges are towards the edges of the quilt and pin to hold in place. Sew with a ¼in seam allowance, leaving the first inch open.

**5** At the first corner, stop ¼in from the edge of the fabric and backstitch. Lift the needle and presser foot and fold. Then fold again. Stitch from the edge to ¼in from the next corner and repeat the turn.

**6** Continue all around the quilt working each corner in the same way. When you come to the starting point, cut the binding, fold under the cut edge and overlap at the starting point.

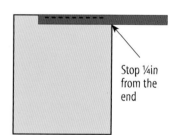

Stop ¼in from the end

**7** Fold over the binding to the back of the quilt and hand stitch in place, folding the binding at each corner to form a neat mitre.

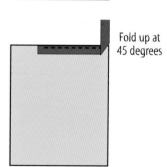

Fold up at 45 degrees

Fold down and stitch from the edge to ¼in from the next corner.

# Making a Larger Quilt

If you want to make a larger version of any quilt, refer to the Vital Statistics of the quilt, which shows the block size, the number of blocks, how the blocks are set plus the size border used. You can then calculate your requirements for a larger quilt.

# Setting on Point

Pick and Mix and Knickerbocker Glory are examples of quilts set diagonally or 'on point'. The patterns contain all the information you need to make the quilt. However, any block can take on a totally new look when set on point and you might like to try one of the other quilts to see what it looks like on point. For this reason we have included information for setting quilts on point. Some people are a little daunted as there are a few things to take into consideration but here is all you need to know.

## How wide will my blocks be when set on point?

To calculate the measurement of the block from point to point you multiply the size of the finished block by 1.414. Example: A 12in block will measure 12in x 1.414in which is 16.97in – just under 17in. Now you can calculate how many blocks you need for your quilt.

## How do I piece blocks on point?

Piece rows diagonally, starting at a corner. Triangles have to be added to the end of each row *before* joining the rows and these are called setting triangles.

## How do I calculate what size setting triangles to cut?

Setting triangles form the outside of your quilt and need to have the straight of grain on the outside edge to prevent stretching. To ensure this, these triangles are formed from quarter square triangles, i.e. a square cut into four. The measurement for this is: Diagonal Block Size + 1¼in
Example: A 12in block (diagonal measurement approx. 17in) should be 18¼in.

Corners triangles are added last. They also need to have the outside edge on the straight of grain so these should be cut from half-square triangles. To calculate the size of square to cut in half, divide the finished size of your block by 1.414 then add ⅞in.
Example: A 12in block would be 12in divided by 1.414 = 8.49in + ⅞in (0.88) = 9.37in (or 9½in as it can be trimmed later).

Most diagonal quilts start off with one block and in each row thereafter the number of blocks increases by two. All rows contain an odd number of blocks. To calculate the finished size of the quilt, you count the number of diagonals across and multiply this by the diagonal measurement of the block. Do the same with the number of blocks down and multiply this by the diagonal measurement of the block.

If you want a rectangular quilt instead of a square one, count the number of blocks in the row that establishes the width and repeat that number in following rows until the desired length is established.

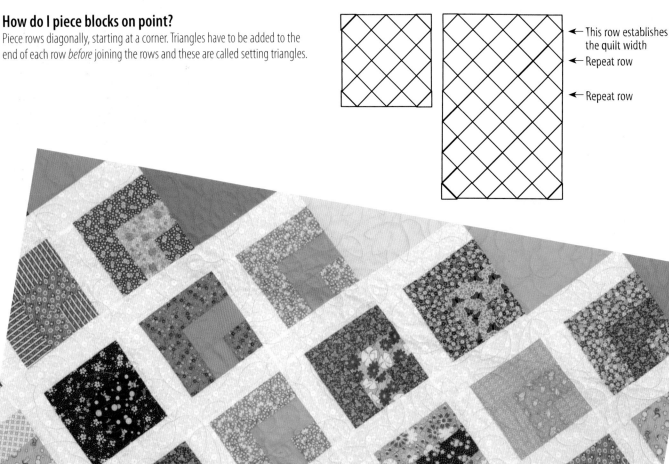

← This row establishes the quilt width

← Repeat row

← Repeat row

# Calculating Backing Fabric

The patterns in this book do not include fabric requirements for backing as many people like to use wide backing fabric so they do not have to have any joins.

## Using 60in wide fabric

This is a simple calculation as to how much you need to buy.
Example: Your quilt is 54in x 72in. Your backing needs to be 3in larger all round so your backing measurement is 60in x 78in. If you have found 60in wide backing, then you would buy the length which is 78in. However, if you have found 90in wide backing, you can turn it round and you would only have to buy the width of 60in.

## Using 42in wide fabric

You will need to have a join or joins in order to get the required measurement unless the backing measurement for your quilt is 42in or less on one side. If your backing measurement is less than 42in then you need only buy one length.

Using the previous example, if your backing measurement is 60in x 78in, you will have to have one seam somewhere in your backing. If you join two lengths of 42in fabric together your new fabric measurement will be 84in (less a little for the seam). This would be sufficient for the length of your quilt so you need to buy two times the width, i.e. 60in x 2 = 120in. Your seam will run horizontal.

If your quilt length is more than your new backing fabric measurement of 84in then you will need to use the measurement of 84in for the width of your quilt and you will have to buy two times the length. Your seam will then run vertical.

# Labelling Your Quilt

When you have finished your quilt it is important to label it even if the information you put on the label is just your name and the date. When looking at antique quilts it is always interesting to piece together information about the quilt, so you can be sure that any extra information you put on the label will be of immense interest to quilters of the furture. For example, you could say why you made the quilt and who it was for, or for what special occasion.

Labels can be as ornate as you like, but a very simple and quick method is to write on a piece of calico with a permanent marker pen and then appliqué this to the back of your quilt.

# Acknowledgments

Pam and Nicky would first like to thank Mark Dunn at Moda for his continued support and for allowing them to use the name jelly roll in the title and throughout this book. Thanks also go to Susan Rogers and the rest of the team at Moda, who are always so helpful and encouraging.

Their thanks also go to Moda for supplying the very generous prize money for this challenge. Thanks also to Singer Sewing Machines for their generous prize of a sewing machine for the winner, and to Winbourne Fabrics in the UK for their donation of prizes to the twelve winning quilters and also for their retailer's prize.

Thanks also go to Jane Trollope and the team at David & Charles for taking up the 'challenge'. It was a new and exciting journey for everyone!

Last but not least, special thanks go to Pam's husband, Nick, and to Nicky's partner, Rob, for their continued love and support.

# About the Authors

Pam Lintott opened her shop, The Quilt Room, in 1981, which she still runs today, along with her daughter Nicky. Pam is the author of *The Quilt Room, Patchwork & Quilting Workshops*, as well as *The Quilter's Workbook*.

Nicky Lintott has been working at The Quilt Room for a number of years and has now taken over the day-to-day running of the business, to allow her very appreciative mother more time to look after her dogs, chickens and now sheep! She also runs the longarm quilting service very successfully.

*Jelly Roll Challenge* is Pam and Nicky's third book for David & Charles, following on from *Layer Cake, Jelly Roll and Charm Quilts* and their phenomenally successful *Jelly Roll Quilts*.

# Useful Contacts

**The Quilt Room**
Shop: 20 West Street, Dorking, Surrey RH4 1BL, UK
Tel: 01306 740739
Mail Order: 37A High Street, Dorking, Surrey
RH4 1AR, UK
Tel: 01306 877307
www.quiltroom.co.uk

**Moda Fabrics/United Notions**
13800 Hutton Drive, Dallas, Texas 75234, USA
Tel: 800-527-9447
www.modafabrics.com

**Creative Grids (UK) Ltd**
Unit 1J, Peckleton Lane Business Park, Peckleton
Lane, Peckleton, Leicester LE9 7RN, UK
Tel: 01455 828667
www.creativegrids.com

**Lecien Fabric**
(European Distributor)
Rhinetex B.V., Geurdeland 7, 6673 Dr. Andelst,
Netherlands
Tel: 31-488-480030
www.rhinetex.com

**Lecien Fabric**
(US Distributor)
The Gary L. Marcus Co Inc, 11 Brownwood Lane,
Norwich, Ct. 06360, USA
Tel: (860) 887 6614
Email: glmarcusco@aol.com
For other countries see Lecien webside:
www.lecien.co.jp

**Daiwabo Co Ltd**
(Japanese Taupes)
For shops and distributor information visit
www.pinwheelstrading.com

**Kaffe Fassett, Heather Bailey and Tanya
Whelan Grand Revival Fabrics**
(European Distributor)
Rowan Yarns, Green Lane Mill,
Holmfirth, HD9 2DX, UK
Tel: 01484 681881

**Kaffe Fassett, Heather Bailey and Tanya
Whelan Grand Revival Fabrics**
(US Distributor)
Rowan Yarns, 4 Townsend West, Suit 8 Nashua,
N.H. 03063 USA
Tel: (603) 886 5041

**Thirties Fabrics by Marcus Brothers**
www.marcusbrothers.com
or Anbo Textiles (European Distributor)
Unit 8–9 Dashwood Industrial Estate, Dashwood
Avenue, High Wycombe, Bucks HP12 3ED, UK

**Reproduction Civil War Fabrics**
Makower UK Ltd, 118 Greys Road, Henley-on-
Thames, Oxfordshire RG9 1QW, UK
Tel: 01491 579727
www.makoweruk.com

# Index